ISRAEL HAS MOVED

ISRAEL HAS MOVED

Diana Pinto

HARVARD UNIVERSITY PRESS

Cambridge, Massachusetts, & London, England

2013

Library of Congress Cataloging-in-Publication Data
Pinto, Diana.
Israel has moved / Diana Pinto.
pages cm
Includes bibliographical references.
ISBN 978-0-674-07342-5 (alk. paper)
1. Israel.   2. Israel—Politics and government.
3. Israel—Social conditions.   4. Israel—Religion.
5. Israel—Economic conditions.   I. Title.
DS102.95.P56 2013
956.9405'4—dc23   2012038241

For my cousins and friends in Israel

CONTENTS

INTRODUCTION

Israel has moved. The country has changed its geographic and temporal references, its political horizons, and its cultural givens. It still occupies, of course, the same GPS geostationary coordinates in the Middle East. However, both mentally and symbolically, Israel has abandoned its Arab neighborhood, whose recent springtime revolutions with their heavy autumnal overtones never really inspired it. Even more important, the country is also in the process of forfeiting its more than 2,000-year-old anchoring—be it in symbiosis or in conflict—within the grand Western symbiosis of Athens, Rome, and Jerusalem.

Israel today thinks of itself as living in its own cyberspace at the very heart of a globalized world with increasingly Asian connotations. It lives inside its own utopia, in the literal sense of a non-place. Its postmodern future is being built on scientific innovation, and yet the country seems to be rooting itself in an increasingly ancient, even archaic, past whose tenets are ever more religiously and ethnically exclusive.

This grand conceptual move, prefigured by many individual geographic shifts, has been taking place silently while the rest of the world (or rather, those who considered themselves friends of Israel) continued to repeat the same old "two-state solution" mantras linked to the peace process. In Israel itself these mantras have lost all relevance, given the absence of political will and the population's desire to look beyond what it perceives—often rightly—as a highly violent and above all in-imical neighborhood.

The contrast between the headlines in the international press in June 2011 and those of the Israeli press was most illuminat-ing on this count. While the international community clung to the smallest official pronouncement or the least concession on the ground to continue believing in the validity of its two-state-solution peace plan, the headlines in the Israeli press were dom-inated by one major problem: the scandalous rise in the price of white cheese, and cottage cheese in particular.[1] The highlight was on the social protests and calls for a boycott of Israel's big dairy industries. The campaign of civic coordination that en-sued brought consumers victory. The price of cheese fell back to normal, if only because the dairies did not know what to do with the mountains of unsold dairy products with their draco-nian expiration dates. Cheap cottage cheese versus peace: the triumph of reality over mirages.

Western observers tend to see Israel as crumbling under un-solvable internal tensions between warring religious, secular, democratic, and nationalist camps. Seen from within Israel, these same tensions are perceived more as familiar background noises, echoes of a search for nostalgic melodies of a time when the country sought to present an idealized image of its progressive Zionist humanism. That type of Zionism could be best conveyed as an impressionist portrait (impressions of Zionism?) of a serene man who had attained the inner calm of full-fledged maturity. Today Israel's self-image is closer to a Cubist painting by Braque or Picasso: a subject that has been decomposed into different clashing planes while nonetheless retaining an intrinsic unity and intensity. One can no longer speak of any harmonious iden-tity. The man is no longer serene, and, to pursue the metaphor, one can ask whether in order to maintain his internal equilib-rium he must not propel himself into a new cult of speed. Futurism has thus replaced Cubism for a country that seems to move forward by running away from itself.

Israel's political classes (both left and right) but also a vast majority of its citizens have understood that the country's stakes and future lie elsewhere: among those powerful emerging nations that, endowed with other historical references, itineraries, and dreams, are beginning to challenge in a Hegelian manner the old Western world—the world that, for better and worse, defined Israel and the most advanced sectors of the Jewish people for the greater part of two millennia. This is no longer the case. The new Israel is no longer haunted by its European past. And even more important, it no longer shares the same intense links with the United States, its long-standing protector and privileged ally.[2] We are now confronted with a different Israel with different identity interests based on different international references and historical hopes.

Israel has abandoned the narrow horizon of its limited kilometers and the abstract hopes of an improbable peace for a new identity best conveyed through fictional Internet addresses: www .israel.org for its highly dynamic and innovative civil society; www.israel.com for its prosperous business world; www.israel .inc for its spectacular technology; www.israel.gov, surely the least impressive of its activities; without forgetting www.israel.god, the most imponderable but also the most loudspoken and vividly present.

The old divisions are thus no longer as pertinent. Their tensions endure but more like verbal jousts. Everyone knows that none of Israel's many identities, including the most extreme, will be able to carry the day. As a result, synergies and parallel existences have taken over, thanks to a cyberspace that unites each tribe at the planetary level, beyond the Israel/Diaspora divisions, which have also become outdated. Globalization and the Internet have thus freed and federated a people that can once again think of itself as a people beyond borders, *precisely* because it lives in symbiosis between Israel and its multiple *elsewheres* at the crossroads of different horizons and cultures.

One should not be mistaken. The Israeli businesspeople who invest in Romanian agricultural lands or build shopping malls in Poland and Central Europe in the highly symbolic heartlands of the old pre-Holocaust Jewish presence—the same lands where pious ultraorthodox pilgrims now flock to revere the tombs of their Hassidic saints—are the same who are also investing in China or in India or in the newly emerging lands of Asia and who will one day invest seriously in Africa and, slowly but surely, albeit indirectly, in those Arab emirates open to them. The world for these Israelis, to refer to Thomas Friedman's metaphor, is indeed "flat."[3] Just as it is for those Lubavitchers who follow the comings and goings of all those globalized and at times lost Jews (most often young Israelis after their military service) in their spiritual quests in India or in Latin America, while opening up new offices in Beijing. Nor should one forget all those adult Israelis who sought and have obtained, without the least historical complex, a European passport thanks to the German, Polish, and now even Baltic nationalities of their ancestors. This does not mean that they feel European, but Europe offers them the possibility of living, traveling, and working throughout the world beyond the constraints of the Israeli village. The number of Israeli intellectuals and academics, often left-wing, as well as artists, managers, and businesspeople who now live outside Israel is constantly growing. Not to mention those former Soviet Jews who have kept at times opaque business ties or even a binationality with Russia, this omnipresent and often indignant mother endowed with such a possessive language. One can truly speak of an Israel outside of Israel.[4]

In brief, the country is on the go and all of this moving is not just symbolic. It evokes the science fiction behind *Star Trek*, and also the possibility of teleporting elementary particles in quantum physics. But in all cases it is important to stress that Israel's conceptual move is perceived by Israel and Israelis as enriching and implies no abandonment of its territorial existence nor loss of an Israeli identity.

Israel thus lives more than ever in its own epoch, but it does so in the context of its own embellished space/time, formed and deformed by centuries of Jewish memory rather than history, and in an elsewhere that no conventional reference to the peace process can possibly perceive. Its space/time is built on the sum of all of Israel's millennial historical experiences, whose validity has been restored by the return to the ancestral biblical lands. In this long-term history, Israel, small and often weak, confronted a succession of hegemonic international actors whose roles could be perceived as both immutable and ever-changing—actors who could very easily take on familiar present-day faces, while resembling all those previous powers who threatened the very existence of the Jews, from the biblical Amalek to Adolf Hitler, and now Mahmoud Ahmadinejad, before disappearing systematically from the historical stage—while Israel, the people and the religion, continued to survive.

In order to understand Israel today, one thus has to adopt a nonlinear postmodern reading. The great biblical and Talmudic past not only has not passed. It is reborn ever stronger before our very eyes. This past now conditions Israel's future, and in so doing it has transformed the very meaning of the term "progress" by pulling it into two contradictory directions. These directions—and this is one of Israel's strengths—have become complementary. On one hand, the term "progress" is carefully applied to technology, medicine, and pure science, all fields where it can take on a neutral connotation. On the other, the term "progress" is invested with a major metahistorical national significance that carries messianic (religious as well as lay) overtones.

What gets lost in this double pull is that old humanistic, social, and cultural definition of universal progress that was the child of European history and became the trademark of Jewish life after emancipation.

The same bifurcation, however, brings Israel closer to those great Asian countries—China being foremost among these—that also oscillate between pragmatic technological progress and metahistorical ancestral readings of their own identity. Above all, it allows Israel to be at the planetary technological avant-garde while also displaying a new pessimism, or at least a lack of hope, at the geopolitical level. Hope, though in a sense that is not really very familiar to us, is now firmly rooted in the ultra-religious camp.

This is why Israel, despite the technology that places it at the heart of the new world economy, can also fold inward, like a Möbius strip. This is no paradox if one defines the country as postmodern. Past, present, and future and above all its own multimillennial tradition are thus bent into a new continuity. It is therefore unnecessary to lose oneself in the welter of daily politics with its alliances and counteralliances stemming from the tensions of the past. In so doing, one would risk missing the essential. New lines of continuity with ancient pasts have emerged. Religious and cultural fundamentals based on a specific Jewish identity have replaced the old, essentially secular and socialist, Zionism of the past. A new community of Jewish interests and values, propelled by planetary horizons along with an egregious economic well-being so distant from our depressed Western contexts, has overcome the old tensions of the past. These have instead been transformed into a continuum of identities—or if one prefers, into a timeless smorgasbord.

The best example of these nuances: the variety of skullcaps *(kippot)* that a growing number of Israeli men are wearing. They go from those made of plain cloth to those that are crocheted (generally used by the right-wing orthodox nationalists) to the black or dark-hued velvet ones worn by the classic orthodox, to the large white ones, almost Muslim in style, worn by many Sephardic Jews, to those that espouse other references (such as the seal of Manchester United or even the aspect of a Matzah, or, for children, characters from cartoon series). The latter are generally bought and worn by visiting tourists, for religion is seldom lived with humor in Israel.

Last but not least, the most important intra-Israeli bond is the modern Hebrew language. One should not minimize its centrality. Nowadays it is spoken daily even by the ultrareligious Jews who in the past used Yiddish, reserving Hebrew solely as the language of prayer. This language, at once biblical and contemporary, is rife with underground labyrinths that have come back to life either because they are diligently excavated or simply because they open up spontaneously and without warning, revealing massive historical and conceptual abysses and new non-Western dimensions. Hebrew has thus become the epistemological glue for Israel's new metahistory. The old political clashes between left and right lose their relevance in such a context. In light of such an ancient/new language and in the context of an ever more pertinent reading of the Bible and the Torah, today's internal political struggles seem very mild indeed, compared to the old biblical fraternal hatreds based on ancestral rage and furor. This is why, behind the very real cleavages inside Israeli society that render it so vibrant and dynamic, new unifying trends have emerged that are deeper and less visible but that condition this new Israel *in motion.*

Conclusion: Israel *farà da se.* For many Israelis, the country has not just moved. It has *moved on:* in the colloquial sense of transcending previous obstacles, the way one "moves on" after a broken relationship, in Israel's case with Europe in the past or with the Middle East in the present. The country has chosen to go forth alone. And why should one doubt it? Luminous towers now pierce the Tel Aviv skyline and their brand new apartments are being sold for prices that have only Hong Kong and London as competition. Meanwhile, on the esplanade that has replaced the city's old dockyards, young adults, iPod earphones glued to their ears, glide by on roller skates, looking like their peers on the Santa Monica boardwalk in California. As for Jerusalem, it has taken on the appearance of a world city, with its luxury hotels, its festivals, its rock concerts, and its opera productions played under the city's ancient walls, which are only rivaled by the operas played at the foot of the Masada fortress— *Aida* in 2011, *Carmen* in 2012. Meanwhile, Eilat exhibits residences where each dwelling has its own private swimming pool, just like Dubai's Palm—but in Eilat there is an economic reality to back this real estate fantasy, which is not based on the mirage of evanescent foreign capital. Nor should one forget the luxurious spas and relaxation centers that now dot Israel's north: perfect examples of a cult of well-being that simply ignores the presence of Hezbollah nearby. The list is long, the national morale euphoric, even though many Israelis, as demonstrated by the tent movement in the summer of 2011, do not profit from this economic wealth.

While the West sinks ever more deeply into its economic moroseness, Israel's rate of growth is comparable to that of the most dynamic Asian countries. In 2010, Israel's military exports amounted to nearly US\$7.2 billion, placing the country among the top four countries in the armaments export field.[5] At the International Aviation Show in Le Bourget in June 2011, the Israeli presence was overwhelming. The country is full of genial ideas quickly translated into start-ups that become world leaders in fields as varied as agronomy, cybernetics, robotics, medical innovations, ecological architecture, and of course the new information technologies. It sounds like a dream, but all this scientific prowess belongs to Israel's daily reality . . . or rather to one of its realities.

Whoever thinks in terms of space/time enters a universe or even a "multiverse" according to astrophysics. But because in the current state of things one cannot really live in cyberspace, Israel cannot really move out of its neighborhood physically—hence the building of security fences against the neighboring Palestinians, and now also along the long, increasingly lawless Egyptian border. The laws of gravity, however, are applicable everywhere and can at any moment bear down on Israel as well. Israel therefore continues to live exactly where GPS situates it, and it should not, like Icarus, risk seeing its dreams shattered by falling heavily into the sea, even one filled with promising gas reserves.

The powerful spatial metaphors are thus radically transformed the minute Israel's terrestrial and daily reality within its geographical bounds is evoked. The country in such a context thinks of itself as an aquarium, as a bubble, or as a tent. These metaphors, which evoke precarious conditions in water, air, and land, speak wonders. They do not really convey the master narrative of Israel as the shelter and the bastion of the Jewish people.

These habitat metaphors are further supplemented by those in the psychiatric realm. Super-Israel at the technological heart of the new world economy suddenly becomes Israel the autistic with Asperger syndrome, the bipolar, the schizophrenic, the paranoiac, the psychotic, and even the psycho-rigid: in other words, an entity that denies the very principle of reality. These are very powerful, even terrifying, metaphors. They are not mine. Israelis from all camps—whether ultraorthodox or extremely secular, young or old, and coming from the most diverse cultural origins—used them freely before me as so many self-evident truths. And I may add, there was not the slightest hint of Jewish humor in their tone.

Deep down, Israelis know there is the other side of the coin behind their country's economic and technological miracle. Almost seamlessly, they then begin talking about their own country as a collective person that badly needs a Jungian psychoanalysis anchored in its own collective symbols. No one is a fool in Israel. Everyone knows that euphoria has a twin: depression. And for depression not to take over the country, there is a third solution: autism. This condition, which occurs among the young (and Israel is both very young as a state and very old as a people), who are often quite brilliant in certain fields, defines those who cannot think of themselves as living in a world populated by others. They do not register the gaze or the emotions of others and are therefore unable to communicate or interact with them, because they do not grasp or understand what might motivate them.

Can one claim that Israel has always been or has become autistic? Many education specialists in the field of Jewish studies and social science and political experts have often resorted to the autistic metaphor in a most casual but also serious manner. They did so probably because in their minds there was also something *positive* and very special, even prodigy-like, in being autistic. And of course psychiatry has a special category to define the autistic intelligent person who can perform incredible mathematical exercises or become a master chess player while being barely able to speak, much less carry on a deep conversation with another person.

This condition could help explain Israel's unique ability to head toward new scientific worlds and to embrace national challenges that it can master on its own. Such autism can also explain Israel's historic relation to its own interiorized God, as well as Judaism's indifference to religious conversion. Any attempt to convert others implies finding the best way to interact with them by penetrating into their deepest values and symbols, fashioning in the process new and attractive symbioses, to which they can adhere—in brief, dialoguing. Autistic personalities rarely dialogue. As with autistic people who feel threatened, Israel can reply to the aggressions of others (in its case most often real and not imagined) only by an excessively forceful and uncontrolled reaction, of which it often becomes its own victim.[6]

In psychotherapy, it is the others who must go toward those who are autistic in order to try to understand them, to stimulate them, and to integrate them. Above all, one should not prove aggressive toward them, much less threaten them. And at all times, one should assume that what the mainstream calls normality is not perceived as such in their universe. We live in an era where, in the West, psychologists and psychiatrists rush to the scene of every terrorist action, any major aggression inside a school, or wherever there has been loss of life, even when due to either a simple accident or a natural catastrophe. Specialists are immediately on the spot to relieve the anguish of the survivors, the collateral victims, and the witnesses, making them recount their experience in extended conversations—the very act of listening offering the best possible therapy.

The Jewish people were never entitled to a friendly ear during all the centuries when they were marginalized, chased from one place to another, and discriminated against, before they were nearly exterminated in Europe. Above all, Jews received no collective psychoanalytical help in the aftermath of the Holocaust. Jewish victims and the Jews as a people rebuilt themselves alone, most often surrounded by silence and what could be called a "hands-off" attitude of the international community. This stance displayed several things at once: guilt and an attendant desire to respect Israel's own will to become fully autonomous, but also— let us be frank—a dose of indifference, antipathy, shame, and malaise that did not make others surround Israel with the necessary care.

When the great powers and the developing countries extended friendship toward the Jewish state, they did so most often based on their own self-interest. The Soviet Union's immediate recognition of Israel did not prevent (on the contrary) Stalin's planned pogrom against the Jews, starting with the trials against the doctors, shortly before the dictator's fortunate death. The help of France and Great Britain during the last years of their colonial policy at the time of the Suez crisis in 1956 transformed itself into a postcolonial coldness, in France's case after the 1967 war, and a new closeness to the Arab world. The emerging countries of Africa displayed a highly volatile gratitude for all the civilian and agricultural help Israel, then a young Socialist state, extended to them. This help was quickly repudiated when their increasingly autocratic leaders turned to the Soviet Union for massive military and political aid. Even the United States, the infallible ally after the 1967 war, displayed often more self-love for its own Pax Americana than love for Israel itself. The result is highly visible today: the protector should have prevented, or at least curtailed, the colonizing of the occupied territories but failed to do so.

As for the hatred of the Arab and Muslim world, and in particular recently the Hamas leadership in Gaza, as well as Iran's own pronouncements, with the constant hyperbolic propaganda of "throwing Israel into the sea," and the use of blood and racial stereotypes dating back to Europe's own ancestral antisemitic fears . . . one cannot imagine a more catastrophic interaction with respect to such a fragile—despite its strength—state with an autistic penchant. The Arab countries who never accepted Israel in their midst did their utmost to aggravate the psychological condition of their neighbor, a neighbor that had fallen on their head without their being responsible for the Holocaust, but whose minuscule territorial presence they should have accepted early on. One should not forget that the Jewish State born on May 14, 1948, was so small and narrow that it did not even reach Jerusalem, a city surrounded by an Arab presence and that was destined to remain international, until the 1949 cease fire finally divided it up between Israel and Jordan.

Autistic: perhaps since its birth, given its unique relationship to its own personal God, but also in the more positive structured sense of its fixation on the Law and God's commandments. The "people apart" survived in a hostile world thanks to its fidelity to the Torah and the Talmud, perceived as self-enclosed documents and arguments. Rich in juridical thought and essentially indifferent to historical interpretations, the Talmud, with its pages framed by an ongoing pluralist discussion among sages across the ages, was the ideal guidebook for Jewish life in exile. For the tensions related in the Torah, between judges and kings and their common chastisement at the hands of the prophets, had lost their terrestrial value to retain a metaphorical message.

Israel today has preserved something of this ancient pedigree, or rather more precisely it has rediscovered it at the level of daily political life.[7] These old ways of reasoning had been politically diluted during emancipation by the power of the Enlightenment. Israel's founding fathers still belonged to a Jewish world that had mingled, after a more or less successful political emancipation, with the other peoples of a Europe that firmly believed in human progress and a better future. This symbiosis has not lasted. Paradoxically, it was destroyed not by the Holocaust, but much later at the end of the 1990s in that double vortex marked by its commemoration and the attendant discovery of the full extent of the horror and the extensive complicity of all countries in its unfolding. This moment unfortunately coincided with the end of the Oslo peace progress and the rise of a new, unexpected antisemitism at the hands of the left and the immigrant Arab world, especially in Europe.

Today the Talmud and the Torah frame the conditions of daily life among ever-growing sections of the population. The Zionists who saw their return to Israel as a secular nation-building enterprise that would give the Jews a normal state, are losing ground to those who think of Israel as a terrestrial messianic entity. In either case, this leads to a country without clearly defined mental or physical borders.

Israel's existential position can be summarized thus: to go forward, always a step ahead while following its own path and destiny, deaf or at least indifferent to the sounds of the world. Israel, more than sixty-five years after the Holocaust, seems to have adopted the attitude that predominated in Jewish life during the two centuries that followed the expulsion of the Jews from Spain in 1492. This attitude can best be summarized as a turning inward toward a closed Jewish community life, the return to religious piety, or for those who are secular, toward an ethnic identity. But above all the return to mysticism and a messianic faith in which religion and the Land are incommensurably intertwined. This time, though, it is not the turning inward of a people inside ghettos, but a turning inward of a State in the process of its own ghettoizing because it is convinced that the world has delegitimized it.

Here too, history offers strange mirrors. In our Western pluralist reading, the isolation of Europe's Jews inside ghettos at the hands of a Church under the impetus of the Counter-Reformation constitutes one of the black pages in Europe's history. But historical research has also demonstrated that seen from *within* the Jewish communities, particularly in the eyes of the religious leaders, this involuntary confinement was perceived not as a major injustice against the freedom of the Jews but as a way of preserving them against external temptations, at least in the Italy of the Renaissance.[8] The story, most likely an anecdote, with its claims that the religious leaders of the Jewish community of Vilna, upon hearing that Napoleon's troops were at the city's doors, proclaimed that it was surely "good for the Jews but terrible for Judaism," only translates the same state of mind with respect to the even stronger temptations of the Enlightenment.

These tensions were supposed to have been eliminated once and for all by the creation of the State of Israel. Instead, they seem to have resurfaced in a new guise. But with one major difference: today in a postmodern age one can turn inward while solidly keeping a foot in the wider world. This is not only Israel's gamble as a state but also the gamble of the ultraorthodox who play hide-and-seek with each new technological advance before finding a way to integrate it into their lives while remaining faithful to their precepts. All of these elements lead me to believe that Israel may be currently in a similar phase, with the old universal values of the Enlightenment slowly retreating in the background, in an expanding world where Western democracy risks becoming just one political option among others.

This distinction brings to mind other international divisions dating back to previous centuries, which back then touched Israel, not as a country but as a "nation" without land. In the seventeenth and eighteenth centuries, Great Britain and the Netherlands, the capitalist nations most open to modernity and that had welcomed Jewish life in their midst, were opposed to Spain and France: the latter had extirpated Jews from its midst, and the former had not yet integrated them. Could Israel today announce or reveal, once again, by its choices and by the way other nations treat it, the dominant values of the decades to come? History does not repeat itself, but sometimes it reverses itself. Israel's mutations today do not bode well for the old Western values of the postwar period: universal human rights, a democratic pluralism that refuses all ethnic nationalisms in the name of an open and full-fledged citizenship, and last but not least an international governance based on supranational laws.[9]

Israel today may have left this constellation. It is happily surfing on the line that separates the declining powers (Europe, but also America, it must be said) with respect to the emerging powers (such as China, India, Brazil, and even, from an Israeli perspective, Russia). The declining powers are still searching for peace in the Middle East and offering solutions that Israel no longer envisages. The emerging powers instead mock such an international interventionism and take Israel as is, totally indifferent to its political and geographic contradictions. What interests them is Israel's strength and hypermodernity. The world's scenario, according to Israel, has thus changed. Visiting Chinese plenipotentiaries are applauded and looked up to with respect while messengers bearing President Obama's good tidings are greeted with icy silence.[10] The protagonists are no longer the same, the musical score beats to other tempos, and the film's message has a different happy end.

In the name of its Jewish identity, is Israel willing to abandon all those old Western notions of democratic progress, goodwill among nations, and the idealistic hopes of world peace? It is of course much too early to know what is illusory and what is real in Israel's moving out into another space/time. But one thing is certain. In its fragile strength and in its strong fragility, Israel has embarked on a massive wager.

1

THE INTERGALACTIC CAFÉ, OR
BEN-GURION AIRPORT

Arriving in Israel is akin to arriving at the intergalactic café in *Star Wars*. Everyone shows up with a clear-cut identity that will not be shed during the stay among others, before returning to his or her world of origin, through separate religious and cultural paths. George Lucas in his café had brought together a vast array of robots, strange birds, hominoids, and other surrealistic creatures. Ben-Gurion Airport in its spacious ultramodernity does the same by welcoming a vast array of humanity, well beyond its Jewish nucleus.

The Israelis, who are only a small minority of the businesspeople on this early June afternoon when I arrive, return to *Eretz* (the "land" in Hebrew, without any need to add Israel to the term). They go through their own police controls when they are not using special machines (which Israel developed and now sells to the world) that read their fingerprints and, soon to come, their irises, to allow them to return home in a few seconds. Their home is generally to be found on the stretch of land that borders the sea from Haifa to Ashdod, via Tel Aviv, the country's economic lung.

We, the foreigners, instead fill a vast hall with so many police lines inching along at very different speeds . . . unless one has a VIP treatment that allows you to clear the barriers, not in Israeli seconds, but in a few short minutes. I have often had this privilege, but did not on this particular occasion, and it is a privilege whose only equivalent can be found in Russia. Back in the normal lines, any border policeman who has the slightest doubt about the purpose of someone's visit can block the line for what seems like ages and can easily last half an hour or more. The line you pick thus gives you access to a bureaucratic lottery, much to the displeasure of my fellow passengers, those French Jews, mainly Sephardic, who feel Israeli at heart and who have family in the country and increasingly own apartments there. They are the first to complain, often in Hebrew, but to no avail. One does not enter Israel easily. If one is a non-Jewish tourist arriving on a first visit, it is best to do so in a group. And this is indeed how most visitors come, with a group leader who stands next to the border police desk to act as an intermediary. And it is while standing in line that one can fully measure Israel's paradoxical nature.

Contrary to other countries, a significant portion of those who arrive in Israel have as their destination not that country, but rather the vast palimpsest of other places that occupy the same physical space as the Jewish state.

Foremost among them, there are the pilgrims who come to the Holy Land from around the world. They are easily distinguishable by the exterior signs they carry: mainly travel bags and hats with the logo of their group accompanied by a prominent cross. Their tour leaders are either Catholic priests wearing a clerical collar and coming from Europe or North America, or wearing the long cassock from Latin America, or Protestant pastors, most often British or German and often dressed as though out for a hike. Otherwise there are the Greek orthodox priests with their black cylindrical toques and their Russian equivalents with slightly different beards and attires. Catholic priests and nuns form their own small groups, as do orthodox nuns, who move about with rapid and somewhat angular gestures, belying in the process their nervousness at having to go through Israel on the way to their convents. Here, in the antechamber of the

Holy Land, these very different children of Christ, each pursuing his or her very special itinerary toward Bethlehem, Nazareth, Jerusalem, and the Galilee, ignore each other, perhaps to better engage in the intra-Christian war over the Saint Sepulchre.

The ultraorthodox Jews instead arrive in the Promised Land. I am surprised to see how most of them enter Israel not as citizens but as foreigners, even when they reside in the country. The passports I manage to glimpse are mainly American and Belgian. It is as if the land in question remained for these highly orthodox Jews a symbolic promise that has to be deserved on a daily basis rather than an acquired and ultimately prosaic reality. If the ultraorthodox women, sporting wigs over their natural hair as an ascribed sign of modesty, all seem to be dressed alike in sober hues spanning only grays, blacks, and browns, their husbands on the other hand are clearly differentiated by the shapes and sizes of their hats, the cuts of their jackets, and whether or not they are wearing knickers, whose style dates back to the eighteenth century, rather than pants. Each detail counts, for it indicates a belonging to different religious and geographic communities whose origins all lie in the ancestral lands of Eastern Europe. Each subgroup clings with a vengeance to its identity in what Freud called the "narcissism of small differences." But these small differences become major divides and take on significant political weight inside the Israeli political setting.[1]

For others, instead, Israel is simply the Land of Opportunity. Filipinos, Thais, Ukrainians, Moldavians, and Poles now arrive in or return to Israel as immigrant workers to fill the service jobs of a country with ever larger needs, since Israel no longer turns to the Palestinians nearby to fill its service sector. These new *Gastarbeiters,* who all possess legal working papers dutifully printed out in Hebrew, will prove to be problematic in the long run, because like their equivalents everywhere else in the world, they will have a tendency to stay on. During the Second

Intifada, several of them were even killed as victims of the suicide attacks in the years 2002–2005. They thus paid the ultimate blood sacrifice of national belonging but without any possibility of becoming Israeli citizens. Their children, however, are attending Israeli schools and speak Hebrew fluently as though it were a self-evident proposition. It is now commonplace in Israel's major cities to see elderly Israelis basking in the sun in the company of their Filipino, Polish, or Ukrainian caretakers, who while sitting on the same park bench with their charges peruse in a distracted manner the local press in Hebrew. These *absolute others* are there to guarantee a dignified, but also ironic, end of the life cycle for elderly Jews, who also belonged to other times and other worlds.

The Russians entering Israel form their own subgroup. It is very difficult to know who they are exactly: Russian Slavs on vacation to see friends or family who emigrated in the last two decades, or simply Israelis of Russian descent traveling back and forth? I remember meeting in Moscow in the early 1990s a non-Jewish Russian whose very first trip abroad had been to Israel, for the simple reason that he had no hard currency. A Jewish friend from Soviet times who had migrated at the onset of Gorbachev's liberalization policies had invited him. The Russian had remained dazzled by Israel but most probably more for its Western wealth than for its Jewish specificity. The Russians queuing in front of me can be either Jewish or non-Jewish, since Israel opened its doors widely to former Soviet Jews, whose Jewish pedigree was often diluted and who have also retained a passionate link to the language, if not to the land. It is hard to know whether they are businesspeople, middlemen in opaque deals, or simple vacationers. The number of young people is impressive. One thing is certain: Russia and Israel continue to be linked by this steady stream of comings and goings.[2]

Noisy and happy, a large group of mainly American and European Jews, all wearing T-shirts with *Taglit* (Adventure in Hebrew) and "Birthright Israel" printed on them, arrive in their Ancestral Land in order to spend three weeks touring Israel in an all-expenses-paid stay financed by the country, backed in turn by generous philanthropists from the Diaspora. The purpose of this program: to bring to Israel young Jews who have never before been to Israel, so that they might discover the country and better understand its problems. The idea is that they will, upon their return to their native lands, become advocates for an Israel that the rest of the world no longer loves. According to *Taglit,* every Jew possesses Israel as an inalienable birthright. The country thus becomes all at once mountain waterfall, torrent, reservoir, stream, river, and estuary of the Jewish identity. But it is also the grand protector who constantly needs to be protected.

This right of return does not please all those who return home in what could be called their Contested Land: those Arab Israelis born in Israel but whose birthright is far more complex, torn as it is between opposing identities. The actress Hiam Abbass, best known for her roles in Israeli films such as *The Syrian Bride* or *Lemon Tree,* has defined the condition of her Israeli Arab peers in the following terms: "We, the Palestinians, live here as if we were in a sandwich, stuck between two peoples and two societies."[3] The mantra of Israel's Arabs who now prefer to call themselves Israeli Palestinians can best be summarized as "I am from here and I won't move" in a quasi-atavistic sense of the term, for their "here" refers to their plot of land and their village.[4] This sense of belonging implies no corresponding feeling of real cohesion (in the usual sense of the term) to a State of which they are peripheral citizens. It is a far older and more visceral sense of belonging. Without doubt, under Israeli rule these Arab and Druze citizens are governed in a far more liberal and benign manner than are their Arab peers or relatives in the surrounding regimes, even after the Arab Spring. But one should not minimize the resignation that accompanies such a partial belonging: that feeling of still being governed by others, after Ottoman and British rule.[5] It is important to underscore that these Arab citizens have never had collective minority rights, except for the recognition of Arabic as Israel's second official language. Israel's current government is trying to abrogate this legal status, thus turning Arabic into a foreign language. Despite this ongoing discrimination, these Israeli citizens—once again a paradox—would never accept out of their own free will to be transferred into a new Palestinian state as part of an exchange in the name of a final peace.

This Arab refusal to leave their lands and villages inside Israel, a not-so-small detail rarely mentioned in international diplomatic discussions, is instead underscored with some pride by official Israelis, who see in it the best proof of the superiority of their own democratic institutions. This may be partially true. But it would be a mistake to draw the wrong conclusions. These Israeli Arabs are moved above all by a static force that in the long run can sap from within the democratic legitimacy of the state . . . if one continues to think in pluralist democratic terms about equal citizenship and individual rights.

And then there are the Asians: Japanese at first, now followed by ever-larger groups of Chinese in the ultimate Exotic Land. Are they Christian? Or simply tourists who having already traveled several times to Europe are now heading to Israel, and in particular to Jerusalem, which is the lynchpin of the Western religious world? I still cannot tell, even after having crossed paths with more than one group of them in the narrow alleys of old Jerusalem. Can they ever understand from the perspective of their Confucian or Shinto serenity that a city such as

Jerusalem can unleash such passionate religious conflicts? These Asian tourists incarnate a new globalized planet, which suits Israel perfectly because, in search of its own inner harmony, it would gladly move into its own autonomous setting.[6]

After having cleared the last police controls, all of these groups, each in its own identity bubble, head out to their own symbolic destinations. But before leaving the airport, they all pass in front of a powerful and extremely moving sculpted head of David Ben-Gurion, Israel's founding father and its first prime minister, whose bearing resembles Rodin's *Balzac*. He goes unnoticed. As do the busts of Gandhi in India, where the visionary of nonviolence no longer holds center stage, aside from the few weeks during the spring of 2011 when the charismatic Anna Hazare went on a hunger strike in his struggle against corruption, a struggle that for a while was followed by India's new middle classes. In Israel, the protest tents over the summer were set up without any reference to Ben-Gurion. The founding father was of no use to the Israeli protesters, who rose up ultimately for pragmatic economic reasons and who did not fight for the return to a more modest and idealistic Israel.

Look up Israel's founder on Google and you will find an article under the very tempting title "David Ben-Gurion: A Brief Biography and Quotes."[7] The text lists Ben-Gurion's statements concerning the Arabs in Palestine. The citations cover a period from the 1930s to the creation of the State of Israel in 1948. They are based, the site says, on declassified Israeli documents and his personal diaries. During this time the Zionist leader envisaged solutions similar to the Turkish-Greek accords of 1922 with their forced and nearly total exchanges of populations, in order to render both countries ethnically homogeneous. The quotes attributed to Ben-Gurion are quite cruel vis-à-vis the local Arab populations. Ben-Gurion wishes them to regroup in what is now Jordan, with Israel occupying the entire west bank of the Jordan River. In brief, one could easily believe that Israel's first prime minister was directly responsible for today's nationalist militants who act on behalf of a greater Israel and against any autonomous Palestinian state.

This interpretation is too simplistic and only partially correct. The site does not offer the least citation from the period after the creation of the Jewish state. After 1948, Ben-Gurion did not just nuance his statements but changed his attitude radically on behalf of the rights of the Israeli Arabs. He also fought mercilessly against the right-wing extremist and Jewish organizations, such as the Irgun, responsible for the terrorist attacks against the British forces in the Mandate years. He was also the elder statesman who criticized openly Israel's occupation of the conquered lands after the Six Day War of 1967 (even though he did want a Jewish presence in Hebron, a city where Jews had lived for centuries before the Arab pogroms of 1929 and 1936). Ben-Gurion's vistas lay elsewhere: he never stopped promoting Israel's development in the vast (all is relative) open spaces of the Negev, where he himself had retired, as opposed to the occupied lands of the West Bank. In brief, Ben-Gurion is the least likely candidate as a guide or mentor for the current nationalist right in Israel. He has been relegated to a purely symbolic presence in a contemporary Israel that has lost its founding references. One of Ben-Gurion's most famous photos shows him chatting amiably with Albert Einstein. The photo was taken in the early 1950s in the United States; Einstein visited Palestine only once, in 1923. Ben-Gurion is thus an icon linked to an entirely different world.

It comes as no surprise that the website fails to offer all of this nuanced information. The English site belongs to a "Palestine remembered movement" while its French counterpart hails under an "International Solidarity Movement" and comes with a Palestinian flag on top. Both sites were launched in 2001 at the height of the Second Intifada. It is not so much its contents, which can be disturbing, but its centrality in the Google listings, which confers symbolic rank and therefore importance to our own perceptions and hierarchies. The Palestinian site on Ben-Gurion pops up on the first search page. One does not have to look for it in less frequented subsequent pages. It brings back to my mind the old advertising in the car rental field when Avis ran a publicity campaign against Hertz on the theme "We are number two. We try harder." The Palestinians are indeed trying harder and with growing international success.

Between this commercial and Hegel's classic philosophical analysis of the link between master and slave, there is precious little to add. The world has moved into multiple new spheres, and the little piece of land that David Ben-Gurion managed to secure and turn into a state for his "people without a land" has become ever more complex.

Last but not least, there is a group of people living in Israel today who have never transited through the airport or for that matter through any port. They are African refugees, mainly from Darfur, and for them Israel is the Land of Safety. They have reached it by foot from Egypt through the Sinai . . . the ultimate historical wink to the biblical Exodus of the Jews. These refugees are problematic, because, having no place to go and not endowed with any recognized Jewish roots, unlike their Ethiopian cousins, they cannot benefit from any clear path into Israeli society. Their swelling numbers have been met with xenophobic and racist reactions from many Israelis and contributed to the government's decision in June 2012 to begin deportation proceedings for those who could be repatriated (those from South Sudan, a brand new state, which has diplomatic ties with Israel). The vast majority of these illegal immigrants, refugees from officially war-torn lands who according to international law cannot be deported, will find a way to hang on at the very edge of an Israeli society increasingly torn between its principles and its ethnic identity.[8] Will they be the last group in this palimpsest of a country? Or just one more layer in a land that is far more geometrically variable than the impressive and oversized airport that carries its founder's name?

2

THE TWO ROADS TO JERUSALEM

Variable geometry begins the minute one leaves Ben-Gurion Airport to head out to Jerusalem. Two equally beautiful highways take you there. Depending on the choice made by the taxi driver, one is confronted either with the seemingly resolved complexity of the past or with the seemingly insoluble contradictions of the present.

Taxi drivers usually take the most classical road, Highway 1, which connects Tel Aviv to Jerusalem. It is an old road, parts of which were traced during the Ottoman era and further consolidated under British rule. This road follows essentially (but with significant exceptions) the curving border established after the 1949 Israeli cease-fire with Jordan, which controlled the West Bank until the Six Day War of 1967. This border is still currently referred to as the Green Line, and theoretically it is the border inside which Israel should withdraw (minus a few lands swaps here and there) should there ever be the kind of peace envisaged by the international community.

The second road, technically speaking Regional Route 443, follows another old Ottoman road, but in reality it is an even more recent highway. It follows a far straighter trajectory toward Jerusalem, almost as the crow flies, but in doing so it traverses what technically are occupied Palestinian lands, on the other side of the Green Line. Officially, and this explains why it is called a regional route, this road is a local road built to connect three new towns—Mod'iin Maccabim Re'ut (inside the Green

Line), Mod'iin Illit (straddling the Line itself) with Kiryat Se-
fer, its ultrareligious neighborhood, on the other side, and Gi-
vat Zeev (squarely outside the Green Line and inside Palestinian lands)—with Jerusalem. All of these towns are inside Israel's
new security fence. This so-called regional route has become
the other way to travel between Jerusalem and Tel Aviv, an indispensable highway without whose existence traffic between
the two cities would grind to a halt.

Highway 1, the most frequented, traverses a legitimate and
even heroic Israel, full of highly important historical sites. A
short distance from the airport, one already penetrates into the
lands of some of the oldest Kibbutzim, set up when the land
was still Ottoman before World War I or during the British
Mandate, well before the creation of the Jewish state. Fruits and
vegetables are still grown on these lands, and under a scorching
sun in early June one can already see the first stacks of hay dot-
ting the fields. In this Lilliputian country, one need not travel
for long before reaching the first greenery with, on the right of
the highway, at the level of Latrun, the Trappist monastery of
Our Lady of the Seven Sorrows. Built in 1890, it housed until
1967 a Lebanese monastic community overseeing the monastery's vineyards, originally planted thanks to the experts who
had established the Rothschild vineyards a few decades earlier.
A little way off, always on the right, one can find the fortress of
Latrun, a major strategic point: from its height it dominates the
road to Jerusalem. In 1948 the soldiers of the brand-new Israeli
army tried in vain to capture the fortress, which the British had
left in the hands of the Arab Legion. The accords of the 1949
armistice with Jordan forbade any shooting against the Israeli
vehicles using the road below on their way to Jerusalem, but
they were seldom enforced. As a result the road below remained
highly unsafe and the Israelis were forced to build a deviation.

This deviation, by the way, is still proposed by Google Maps as an alternative to Highway 1.

The Latrun fortress became Israeli only after the Six Day War victory. The no-man's-land that surrounded it was integrated into Israel proper, with the evacuation of several Arab villages as collateral damage. The fort today houses the Israeli army's tank corps museum. At the bottom of the hill, one can still see the preserved remains of several burned jeeps and tanks—the last witnesses to the battles that a still-small Israel, in its heroic phase, waged against the Jordanian authority.

Were it not for these few jeeps, the unknowing visitor could never guess the complex history that unfolded at Latrun. The history was initially glorious for the Arabs and tragic for the Israelis, who during the 1948–1949 war risked being entirely cut off from Jerusalem. To add to the original Israeli tragedy, many of the soldiers who lost their lives at Latrun were young Holocaust survivors from the concentration camps. After 1967, the history became glorious for the Israelis and humiliating for those who would become either Israeli Arabs or Palestinian refugees. In both cases, their presence is largely forgotten, as one continues to drive along a highway, which like all the highways of the world gives the impression of being devoid of any history.

This past fraught with heroism and pain on both sides is now hidden behind the lush vegetation of a hilly national park. Its trees were planted thanks to a highly organized "plant a tree" national campaign that had Jews around the world contribute for decades to the greening of Israel by offering individual trees or clumps of trees to celebrate the birth of a child, a bar or bat mitzvah, or a retirement, or to commemorate the death of a loved one. One is surprised to see a vast impressive dark green forest dominate the horizon on the way to Jerusalem, despite the tiny proportion of the country.

By turning one's head to the left, instead, the new town of Mod'iin Maccabim Reut, about twelve kilometers to the north of Latrun, appears on the horizon. Ideally situated halfway between Tel Aviv and Jerusalem, planned to offer housing to young families who could not afford the exorbitant prices of Israel's most important cities, Mod'iin, which in its main neighborhoods is inside the Green Line, is a legitimate Israeli town and home to more than 100,000 residents. But on the other side of the Green Line, the town is in effect contiguous with its less legitimate sisters, which use Route 443.

Highway 1 continues its slow ascent toward Jerusalem by reaching, on the right, the Arab village of Abu Gosh, which is announced by highway signs in both Hebrew and Arabic. This Israeli Arab village was one of the preferred exotic places for those Jewish residents of Jerusalem who did not observe the Shabbat. They could enjoy a pleasant Saturday break in Abu Gosh restaurants, which remained open and offered a good Ottoman meal. I do not know whether this tradition continues. Jerusalem now has gourmet restaurants that serve an excellent planetary cuisine, including nonkosher food, even oysters and lobsters. The constraints of the Shabbat, increasingly respected by an ever-growing number of orthodox Jews, still remain optional, even though there are frequent and well-publicized fights between the two worlds. The bilingual Hebrew-Arab signs indicating Abu Gosh on the highway make me realize that inside Ben-Gurion Airport all the signs are in Hebrew and in English, without the least reference to Arabic. This is the best proof that Israel's airport has already left its GPS position to move into its own space, well before the current government's wishes to remove Arabic as the other official language.

With the final ascent toward Jerusalem, all traces of greenery disappear. The surrounding hills become grey-beige witnesses to the area's massive aridity, but they now lack the beautiful accompaniment they possessed in biblical times: olive trees. The trees have been sacrificed to make way for banal rows of new houses whose ecological cost is surely catastrophic, but whose political repercussions are even more so, since they are built on what is considered Palestinian land by international law. And then finally, with one last ascent, one reaches Jerusalem proper: on the right one can see the vast modern Jewish cemetery, the hospitals, the vast turnabouts, the central bus station, and just before reaching the residential neighborhoods, a gleaming new Bridge of Chords (meant most probably to evoke a harp— perhaps even David's), which one recognizes instantly as the work of the Spanish architect Santiago Calatrava. In our time, any self-respecting world city boasts one of his bridges, and Jerusalem, which does not have the faintest stream running through it, is no exception to this planetary fashion.

But let us return to Highway 1 in terms of its most mundane aspect: its monstrous traffic. During peak hours, cars and trucks are practically at a standstill in a never-ending bottleneck. The authorities have tried to widen some portions of the highway, but this has proven to be a near-impossible task, given the minuscule land at stake and the complex topography that unites but also separates Jewish and Arab villages. Furthermore, Israeli ecologists have fought long and hard against any encroaching on the natural reserves and parks. As a result, Israel was forced to adopt solutions that place it among the avant-garde nations in terms of ecological highway building. They have come up with a brilliant solution consisting of tunnels and bridges that allow the parks' protected animals, small and big, to transit from one protected area to another without incurring any danger from passing cars.

But what happens when this ecological reasoning is applied to Israeli-Palestinian relations? Regional Route 443 offers a most revealing answer. If one searches on Google Maps, the grand geographical arbiter in cyberspace, for all possible itineraries between Tel Aviv and Jerusalem, Route 443 is not listed. For an obvious reason: it cuts across non-Israeli Palestinian land. But beyond its geographical provocation, this route incarnates perfectly the schizophrenia of Israel's recent history.[1]

The route was conceived during the years of hope linked to the Oslo peace process. The army had justified to Israel's Supreme Court the construction of the highway through Palestinian lands by pleading that it would benefit above all those Palestinians who went to work in the Tel Aviv region. The highway in its original design thus incarnated all the hopes for peace: one exit leading to Ramallah, the other leading to the original town of Mod'iin Maccabim Reeut. But there was one slight problem with this vision: the Palestinians whose life was purportedly to be facilitated by the route did not share this reading. For them, Israel was simply building on their land. It was thus no accident that Route 443 became one of the crisis points during the Second Intifada, when young Arabs from the adjacent villages began throwing stones and Molotov cocktails at the passing Israeli cars. At the height of the Intifada, three Israeli soldiers who were trying to join their military base took the wrong exit and were taken prisoner by some militants. They were then brought to a Palestinian police station and savagely murdered. Route 443 was closed in order to create security checks and protective barriers, and the idea was to reopen it only to Israeli cars. All references to the original pro-Palestinian reasons for its construction disappeared. Today, the Palestinians are, for most Israelis, an unwanted presence on the road, one that must be constantly limited and controlled. The real purpose of the route is no longer cloaked in the rhetoric of peace. The road is there to service the new Israeli settlements and communities built on what still remains technically Palestinian land. The route thus leads to smaller closed routes protected by protective fences, officially called "service roads." These can be used only by Israeli settlers and of course the army, which is there to protect them.

The highway that dares not call itself so still carries the stigmata of the response to the Second Intifada. Military checkpoints, one in the direction of Tel Aviv, the other in the direction of Jerusalem, control access to the legitimate portion of the highway inside the Green Line. The portion of the road that services Ramallah is to be found between these two checkpoints. Israeli activists petitioned and won before the Israeli Supreme Court, which ordered the reopening of the road to Palestinian traffic in 2009. But in order for the Palestinians from the Ramallah side of the road to communicate with their own Arab villages on the other side of Route 443, special tunnels (no bridges) were built—reminiscent of the ecological tunnels along Highway 1. And along entire portions of Route 443 one can see tall walls that bear an uncanny resemblance to those designed as sound barriers in most other parts of the world. Here, instead, the barriers have been erected to prevent Palestinians from the nearby villages from throwing rocks and other projectiles onto the passing cars. Elsewhere barbed wire fences prevent any local access to the road.

In other words, this highway is the perfect reflection of the current atmosphere of nonpeace. The apparently insurmountable tensions that underlie it could also be perceived as an ongoing double war of attrition, a war in which the only real goal for both sides is to hang on until the other side cracks.

Highway 1 offers a stunning spectrum of geographical nuances as it winds through cultivated fields, vineyards, and forests before reaching the dry Jerusalem hills. Route 443, the highway that does not dare to say its name, after traversing the very last cultivated fields inside the Green Line, whose name for once really makes sense, is immediately surrounded by a countryside whose beauty and harshness is quintessentially biblical. In the intermediate area at the heart of Palestinian land, there are virtually no traces of a human presence on hills where rocks and olive trees have coexisted for millennia in pastoral silence. At the top of some hills, one can see a few Arab villages with their minarets. The few modern concrete houses at the bottom of the hill in no way disturb the timeless architecture of these villages. Their names do not adorn the slightest billboard on the highway, for the simple reason that no highway exit leads to them. They seem to float above the biblical rocks as so many mirages of a distant time—a time before Israelis, with their Western impulses and their desire to build houses and to till the land, transformed the very aspect of this land/palimpsest. In front of such a contrast between civilizations, in the deepest and most ancient sense of the term, I can only think of Cain and Abel, Jacob and Esau: their rivalries, their jealousies, their heritages. Who decreed that this pastoral world with its austere and metaphysically splendid hills did not possess its own logic and dignity? Why did it have to be replaced by hills turned into suburbia? The abyss does not just cut across Israeli-Palestinian relations but runs far deeper as a gash over the very nature of time.

Only the Ramallah skyline, which one can catch a glimpse of on the left, possesses a host of modern buildings, even an entirely new neighborhood, as though it had succumbed to the virus of Western modernity. It is no accident. The Western powers see in Ramallah's alleged modernity a promising sign for the future. They rejoice in this Palestinian economic dynamism and creativity and see in it the underpinnings of the future Palestinian state, whose coffers are constantly being refilled by the international community in the hallowed name of the two-state solution. But can all of this Western momentum replace the will of the Palestinians to live with their own rhythm and in their own space/time?

Route 443 still holds two other sore spots in store. The first, not really visible from the highway, is the Khalandia checkpoint: the compulsory crossing point that allows Palestinians to reach (or rather, not to reach) Jerusalem, or rather their East Jerusalem. They can do so only after having transferred from one taxi to another or stepped down from a bus to take another often a few hours later. There is no need to describe the stress, the fatigue, and the often-tragic circumstances under which young soldiers will or will not allow the Palestinians to circulate between towns and villages. Israeli Jewish journalists from *Haaretz* do so far better and more methodically and in far harsher condemnatory tones than any foreign journalist.[2] Israeli human rights activists and members of nongovernmental organizations, such as B'Tselem, stand at the checkpoints to try to facilitate, by their sheer presence, the smooth handling of urgent cases. But one must in all fairness stress that the Palestinians themselves are in part responsible for Israeli suspicions and toughness at the checkpoints: many of them during the Second Intifada used ambulances to transport fighters disguised as sick or wounded passengers, along with their arms and bombs.

A bit farther down the road is the second sore spot: Ofer Prison, which unlike the checkpoint is highly visible, since it is surrounded with barbed wire and flanked by a grey concrete surveillance tower decorated with a large blue Star of David. The association with other historical towers, other barbed wires, and other pasts—however false—is unavoidable. Ofer is both a prison and a military tribunal. Palestinian prisoners guilty of acts of terrorism or of violence, with or without murder, are imprisoned there, and it is also there that they are judged, in what is often an expeditious manner.

And then the final ascent toward Jerusalem. This entrance into the city is heralded by the ultraorthodox settlements, built beyond the Green Line and now encircling the city. They too, like the Arab villages, have a mirage quality to them, but in this case only to evoke a far too dense and prosaically functional urban monotony. Those who dwell in these settlements could not care less. They live for the Talmud and their time is millennial. But in more prosaic terms, these ultraorthodox couples have extremely large families, ranging from half a dozen to a dozen children apiece, and in the worldview of their spokesmen it is self-evident that their settlements must expand. The settlers need ever more kindergartens, schools, synagogues, and houses to accommodate this vertiginous demographic spiral. Here we are at the very heart of the "construction versus freezing of the settlements" issue with its constant headlines in the world press.

It is hard not to admire the sheer collective perseverance of these ultrareligious settlers, whose families before the Holocaust were historically far smaller in size, in their current determination to bring to life more Jews to somehow replace those who were murdered . . . if only they would do so not on these contested lands and in the name of ever more intolerant beliefs.

As one reaches Jerusalem, the highway becomes strikingly beautiful in a modern manner. It has been carefully landscaped to highlight rows of young olive trees and other bushes, which stand out from the golden soil like so many works of art. These olive trees are most elegant: tall and straight and planted just right in terms of a perfect avant-garde urban design. They have nothing in common with the ancient gnarled and metaphysical olive trees, which the Israelis have chopped down and continue to chop down in their quest for ever-larger expanses of urban land, to the detriment of the Palestinian villagers and their time-honored fields.

The highway ends to become the Menachem Begin circular road in an ironical twist of history. The ring road was meant to honor Begin, the architect, along with Anwar el Sadat, of the Israeli-Egyptian peace accords, brokered by President Jimmy Carter in 1979. The result was over thirty years of peace with Egypt. But nowadays, confronted with the new uncertainties stemming from the Arab Spring, particularly in Egypt, one can wonder whether the new Israel, increasingly closed within itself, would rather honor with this ring road not Begin the prime minister but Begin the old terrorist leader of the Irgun, the organization that was responsible for the terrorist attacks against the British Mandate forces, and the man who never believed in or wanted the creation of a Palestinian state.

It is not so far-fetched to recall this distant past. It is coming back in a revisionist vein. The press in June 2011 was full of articles announcing that the Netanyahu government was planning to lift up the remains of the *Altalena,* the ship carrying arms on behalf of the Irgun, which the newly minted leader of Israel, David Ben-Gurion, had the army sink in 1948 as one of the very first acts of responsible government of a sovereign Israel.[3]

But let us return to Route 443. The rare taxi drivers that take it generally do so in a tense silence. I have the impression they try to guess their passenger's identity before choosing to use this road. My chauffeur is a native-born Israeli of Moroccan origin. He speaks excellent English, which he perfected through numerous stays in the United States. His first question upon greeting me at the airport was to ask me whether this was my first trip to Israel. When I reply laughing that this is really not the case, he looks at me in the rear-view mirror and swerves toward Route 443, while announcing that he always takes this road. I am not at all sure that he is being truthful.

I have arrived on the eve of Jerusalem Day (the holiday that commemorates the reunification of the city at the hands of the Israeli army after the Six Day War of 1967). Route 443 is packed with cars with Israeli flags glued to their windows or that, football fan style, are flying them out of the window. On this day, such flag-driven patriotism is not entirely innocent. When we reach the part of the highway that runs through Palestinian lands, I ask my driver, pretending not to know the answer, whether we have indeed arrived in the "contested areas." He shakes his head and, pointing to the hills that surround us, tells me in a surly but also jaded manner: "Yes, indeed, we are not allowed to build here." The angry tone with which he conveys this information is exactly the same any real estate agent would use in front of choice land that is zoned, for the time being, outside his purview.

I then ask him the names of the Arab villages that surround the highway. He gives them to me in a distracted manner, as if I were asking a boring question, such as the full geological name of nearby rocks. And then he tells me, as if he were picking up again a sentence left hanging in the air, but one that was never begun in reality, that "everyone was infinitely better off before the Second Intifada," when one could circulate freely throughout the land. Back then, my driver, who is in his mid-fifties, tells me, he could visit his Arab employees (he used to run a small transport company), who were also his friends, in Ramallah and Hebron. He certainly has a point there, but it is not a promising point for any future two-state solution. Politics has destroyed such a simple one-sided vision . . . and he should know, he who survived one of the terrorist attacks in the Hillel Café in Jerusalem. Arik, for everyone is on a first name basis in Israel, relates this story in a very calm manner during our fourth trip together on Route 443 between Tel Aviv and Jerusalem, for he has become my semi-official chauffeur as I shuttle between the two cities to give lectures. He is also quick to point out that his Arab friends all came to visit him in the hospital . . . but, he sighs, that was before the protective barrier was built. Meeting them now has become virtually impossible, for they can reach Jerusalem only if they are driving an ambulance; and this by definition means that they have little time to spare for any socializing. And then he adds, smiling, that he does indeed have problems clearing security portals in airports, because the surgeons left one piece of shrapnel inside him, for it was too close to the abdominal wall.

And then, turning to me, since I of course sit up front in the car with my new friend, he starts to praise the American Congress for the lavish welcome and standing ovation they gave to Prime Minister Netanyahu during his trip to the United States in May 2011—a subtle way of showing contempt for Obama, the failed American president in many Israeli eyes. Arik is no extremist. He conveys Mediterranean warmth and kindness; he is a proud patriot with a moderate tone. But his Zionist dream has little in common with those of the Ashkenazi founding fathers in the early years of the state. His father, a poor Moroccan immigrant, was a pro-Begin laborer who had major problems with the Zionist East European dominated trade unions, who refused to accept him as one of the elected workers at his plant. He belongs to the new free-enterprise Israel, loves America, but would not dream of ever moving there. Europe is a fine place to visit. But Israel is his sweet biblical homeland.

The last chauffeur to have taken me to the airport along Route 443 is of an entirely different mettle. First of all, he is driving a private limousine that has been hired by the organizers of the Presidential Conference to bring participants from the airport to Jerusalem and back, and I sit in the backseat as expected of me, for I am a "VIP." Young, wearing a knitted kippah, which usually denotes nationalist inclinations, speaking a barely functional English, he has the body language of a guy who does not shy away from tough confrontations. As we pass by Ofer Prison, in front of which a few Israeli human rights activists regularly plead on behalf of families who hope to see their sons get a fair trial, he points to the prison and snarls, "Over there, the 'Four Seasons,' " his way of defining the prison as a luxury hotel. The night before, at the closing session of the Presidential Conference, Prime Minister Netanyahu had announced, after the Hamas government in Gaza had refused to allow the Red Cross to visit Gilad Shalit, the kidnapped soldier, in his prison, that henceforth Arab prisoners accused of terrorism would no longer be able to pursue their studies or benefit from other democratic privileges while in prison. The threat proved hollow; a few months after my trip the prime minister agreed to free most of these prisoners as part of the deal that allowed Gilad Shalit to be freed on October 18, 2011, after five years of imprisonment. I dare mention to the driver that the title "Several Seasons" for the prison would be more appropriate, to convey the length of imprisonment of detainees, who are mainly activists rather than terrorists. But my driver is not listening; his ears are glued to the soft music being played on the radio, and even if he were, he would not grasp the irony in my remark. He has only contempt for an outside world he considers as inherently hostile.

In his own way, he is the perfect alternate to the VIP chauffeur who brought me to Jerusalem from the airport during my second June stay, but this time using Highway 1. He was a university student who spoke quite good English and who told me proudly that he was born in Ariel, one of oldest Jewish towns built on the other side of the Green Line. He spoke warmly of his childhood in this town, which in his eyes was just as legitimately Israeli as Tel Aviv or Ashdod. I realize that for his generation, the very concept of the Green Line is surely the equivalent of the French Maginot Line at the beginning of World War II: a fortified defense border that turned out to be totally inefficient in holding off the enemy, the very symbol of a defective strategy.

It is not necessary to be young and religious or born in the occupied territories to subscribe to such a reading. Secular left-wing professors from Tel Aviv University shared the same feelings when they pointed to the hills standing out beyond the Tel Aviv horizon to announce that theoretically these hills would be in the "other state" if the two-state solution were to be implemented at the hands of the international community. "Continue talking away," they seem to imply, "but you are not the ones living here." One of the professors gives me a little tour of the city, pointing out those areas that used to be small Arab villages in the past (some of them even after the creation of the Israeli state in 1948). I gaze in the direction in which he has pointed his finger, but all I can see is a residential neighborhood full of towers, gardens, and playgrounds. Memory has become an academic pursuit. Not the slightest trace of an Arab past has been preserved.

I finally understand that in the long-term vision of Israel's new moderates (far more to the right than the moderates of yore), the highway that still hides behind the name Regional Route 443 is destined to become the equivalent of Highway 1: a long asphalt ribbon traversing a harmonious new Israel full of new towns and even a few quaint Arab villages (inside the protective barrier), which will with time become picturesque. These little Arab hamlets will no longer contain the dynamic new generations; these will have moved (at least, according to Israeli wishes) to Ramallah to build their own state, on the other side of the protective barrier, where empty hills will await them.

This rather moderate and calm vision—at least compared to the projects cherished by the ultra greater-Israel nationalists who want all Arabs to leave the West Bank—was explained to me in full detail from the esplanade of East Talpiot, one of the most powerful and startling memoryless historical sites I have ever encountered.

3

THE LESSON FROM EAST TALPIOT

The yellow helmet with blues stripes surely covers a black kippah, because sidelocks *(payot)* are sticking out of it and floating in the wind next to a reddish-brown beard. The young man looks a bit ill at ease as he stands upright on a Segway, those strange two-wheeled contraptions endowed with a gyroscope that allow their users to circulate at a faster clip than by merely walking, and to go forward or backward by simply moving their bodies in the right direction. Entire packs of helmeted tourists, most often American, circulate in Paris and its formal gardens on such vehicles.

The young man in question, however, is not a tourist. He is at home in his own holy city of Jerusalem. His long black coat, worn even in the day's torrid heat, along with his white shirt define him as an ultraorthodox Jew. I wonder where he has left his large black hat. His wife is not holding it. She too is standing on a Segway, her feet barely showing under her long black skirt, and she is sporting a light-blue helmet not unlike those worn by the United Nations forces. The helmet just as surely hides the wig she must wear as a very observant Jew. A young man with a backpack stands in the middle between the two. He is dressed casually in blue jeans, T-shirt, and a baseball cap. Ray-Ban sunglasses complete this Californian outfit. He is in charge of the Segway fleet, and he is busy trying to explain to the couple how one navigates these strange childlike scooters. Totally indifferent to the tourists who are photographing them, given the uncommon nature of the moment, they listen carefully to his instructions. Their bodies, and surely also their education, are still too rigid to allow the Segway to move forward . . . for the time being.

The friend with whom I observe the scene and who is a researcher in a policymaking institute, observes the couple with displeasure. He does not like their venturing into the world of frivolous leisure activities. The Segway, he tells me, is not a useful transportation vehicle, but an object straight out of that consumer world that ultraorthodox Jews should be shunning. He should know. He too is ultraorthodox and wears the seemingly compulsory black suit and white shirt, replete with the prayer *Tallit* under his shirt. I realize he is not wearing a large black hat either, but just a black velvet *kippah*. He explains to me that he does not wear a hat but on Shabbat wears a *Shtreiml,* that large fur hat that ultrareligious Polish Jews had taken on, along with breeches, from the fashion world of the Polish nobility in the seventeenth and eighteenth centuries. He expects me to laugh in secular mockery, especially because he is a Jew whose family is of Tunisian origin and whose rabbinical forefathers knew nothing about fur. But my smile contains a hefty dose of admiration for such traditions, which seem outlandish in 40° Celsius weather but which incarnate ironclad principles. The young man on the Segway may or may not belong to my friend's brand of ultraorthodoxy. Minor sartorial differences count significantly in this black-and-white ultrareligious world whose uniforms are as complex as those of Europe's nineteenth-century regiments.

Watching the Segway couple, I am reminded of the comments of an eminent specialist in Jewish philosophy, Avi Ravitsky, who used to explain that Israel as a state could never have come into existence without a fundamental but also counternatural religious/secular compromise, spearheaded by two grand figures:

David Ben-Gurion, on the one hand, and the followers of Rav Abraham Isaac Kook, the ultraorthodox chief rabbi of British-mandated Palestine, who died in 1935, on the other.[1] Rav Kook's followers, namely the Hazon Ish, according to Ravitsky, accepted the Zionist creation of the Jewish state even though Orthodox Judaism had always stipulated that such a state could reappear only with the coming of the messianic times. For Kook and his disciples, despite their ostensible secular agenda, the Zionists were vital instruments of God working, unknown to themselves, toward such a messianic goal. Ben-Gurion chose to include the ultraorthodox inside Israel's state system by according them special privileges, such as subsidized Yeshiva training and exemption from military service for their young men. Israel's first prime minister perceived the ultraorthodox as anachronistic Jews destined to disappear, but he felt they were entitled to live out their collective existence in dignity under the auspices of the Israeli state, given their near extermination during the Holocaust.

Ravitsky liked to repeat that the two camps made their respective compromises even before the official birth of the state because they were both convinced that their camp would inherit the grandchildren of the other.[2] As I contemplate the crowds of ultraorthodox in Jerusalem today, I feel that even Rav Kook would have been surprised by the excessive (in terms of rigidity) degree of his victory . . . even though his own son, Rav Tzvi Yehuda Kook, was the founder after the 1967 victory of the ultranationalist Gush Emunim (Bloc of the Faithful), which promoted religious settlement of the West Bank, relabeled as "Judea and Samaria." But might not this total religious victory still turn out to be Pyrrhic in the end?

Will the young couple on their Segways defect to the other side? Many liberal and secular Jews are convinced that a number of these ultraorthodox young men and women, who live surrounded by numerous brothers and sisters, will sooner or later let themselves be won over by the sirens of modernity. If that were to be the case, they would simply be reproducing a time-honored pattern of social mobility. The ultraorthodox East European *Shtetls* were the reservoir from which progressive and even revolutionary European and later American Jews moved out into the world. But today nothing is less certain. These young ultraorthodox couples can live postmodern lifestyles (Segways *and* strict religious observance) without necessarily betraying their camp. Family demographics, besides, play in their favor.

In Israel today, the Kook–Ben-Gurion wager has taken on an entirely different aspect. The two camps are beginning to fuse at least partially. Highly visible skirmishes between extremists on both sides continue to seize media attention, even internationally, particularly when it comes to infringing or curtailing women's rights (such as requiring women to sit in the back of some Jerusalem city buses), in a seeming replay of the civil rights struggles in America in the late 1950s and early 1960s.[3] But nothing in Israel is ever that simple. The country boasts women who are starred generals, and most ultrareligious Jews condemn such fundamentalist extremes worthy of the Salafists or the Taliban. Besides, Jewish ingenuity is always coming up with practical solutions to even the most extremist ultrareligious demands. The latest find: "modesty glasses." Men can now add special blur-inducing stickers on their lenses that, while allowing them a few meters of clear vision so that they can walk safely in the streets, blur the rest of the world so that they need not see immodestly dressed women.[4] The solution may seem strange but it is philosophically admirable, compared to the tactics of Islamic extremists. Rather than insulting or lapidating immodest women, Jewish extremists have simply decided to remove them from their field of vision.

More to the point, the ultrareligious (above all the modern orthodox, and not so much the Haredim) today are increasingly consenting to the education of their daughters in Jewish terms by creating special Yeshivas for women, where they too can delve into the deepest spheres of Talmudic learning. Highly orthodox Jewish women in the past always studied practical subjects, if only to be able to maintain their husbands during their lifelong Torah studies. For the time being, women are not allowed to study with or to share their Talmudic knowledge with men beyond their husbands, but no one can prejudge the future inside an orthodox world that has managed to survive all dangers.

Above all, confident in their numbers and in their political power, and perhaps in an effort not to rock the Israeli boat too far, some ultraorthodox rabbis are now encouraging their young men to work. Such a revolution would only mark a return to older times, when only the most brilliant and creative Talmudic scholars had the privilege in Europe and in America to spend their entire lives studying. To do so they were often supported by a local philanthropist or by the family of their Rebbe, whose daughter they often married. The vast majority of all other Yeshiva students stopped studying when they reached their level of competence and began working, often in the most humble trades, in order to support their families. Ben-Gurion and Kook's followers, through their compromise, played a key role in subsidizing ultraorthodox students, allowing them to study well beyond their intellectual capacities. They essentially offered them the most luxurious of welfare state subsidies.

This all-too-comfortable situation drew particularly strong criticisms from those who supported the tent movement in the summer of 2011: members of the middle class protesting against the rising cost of living and furious that the ultraorthodox were being subsidized for their Yeshiva training. A writer of the stature of Amos Oz in a letter of support for the tent protesters considered the settlements and the ultraorthodox Yeshivas responsible for the growing state deficits and accused them of producing "generations of ignorant bums, filled with contempt toward the state, its people and 21st-century reality."[5] His were the words of an aging Cicero nostalgic for a pure and hearty pioneer Israel that sought to bring normality to the Jewish people. Hope had changed camps and now belonged to those who, buttressed by a religious vision, considered Israel as endowed with a very specific mission. The tent movement did not live up to Amos Oz's hopes, for it did not transform Israel's social and economic priorities. Despite the financial hardships of many of its citizens, the country basks in its economic growth—echoes of Asia, including in its low unemployment figures.

Just as significant, the ultraorthodox are no longer lagging behind. They now consent, in increasing numbers, to send their sons into newly created special units inside the army, where they are given time to pursue their Talmudic studies, in an all-male environment and with superkosher food. The first ultraorthodox combat battalion was created in the summer of 2011 to be stationed on the Golan.[6] And there is good reason to believe that the ultraorthodox world is slowly opening up to a "closed" Internet in their family lives. Many ultra-orthodox young women are also beginning to work in the computer services industry in specially designed all-female contexts.

The Ben-Gurion–Kook issue of who would be inheriting the children of the other no longer seems so relevant. A metaphor comes to mind: that of the DNA double helix. Israel's two founding currents are currently recombining to produce a new Israeli reality that lives in its own space/time. And this new Israel does not have much in common with the old country, which was proud of its ultrasecular and valorous army, *Tsahal*, the child prodigy of the Ben-Gurion camp. Will these ultraorthodox artillery soldiers and officers, who pray with their *Tefillin* prayer straps on their head and who wear their *Tallit* prayer shawls over their uniforms and their *Tzitzit*, knotted shawls underneath, and who live in their all-male units, use a closed Internet, and fervently believe in the religious sanctity of their greater Israel, still be Western? Or will they increasingly resemble Chinese troops? It is difficult to believe that they will ever obey any order to dismantle the slightest settlement beyond the Green Line, be it on the most remote hill of Judea and Samaria, even when composed of a single camping car. Bringing such ultraorthodox young men into the Israeli army can thus be an equivocal goal. On the one hand, they would become full-fledged Israelis involved in all spheres of national life. On the other hand, by their sheer religious demands, they risk upsetting the army's traditional openness and career opportunities, particularly with respect to women.[7]

The Segway riders, my ultraorthodox friend, and I are all standing on the East Talpiot esplanade. This is a favorite tourist destination. From there one enjoys a stunning view of the Old City of Jerusalem with the Dome of the Rock at the center, the Temple Mount right behind, and a bit farther to the right the newly built separation fence that snakes its way through the hills at the edge of the Judean desert. My friend, it turns out, had brought me here with a purpose. I am on a field trip of sorts, and he is about to give me a "hands on" geopolitical lesson. Seen from Talpiot, the minute size of the field—or is it a theater?—is simply startling, even for someone who is acquainted with its stakes.

I should specify that my friend brought me to East Talpiot only after enquiring about my ties to Israel. I had told him that I had never personally considered Zionism to be a valid life choice for me, that I criticized Israeli politics, but that at the same time I could not conceive of a world without Israel. But above all I had told him that regardless of what the distant future might bring, the sheer coming together of so many Jews in one place has produced not only the renewal of a language and a religion, but also an intellectual and cultural renaissance. The fruits of this revival, I suggest, will recharge the batteries of the Jewish people for centuries to come.

My friend greets my words with massive enthusiasm. Clearly what I have said must echo, albeit very superficially, some major Kabbalistic interpretation of the world that he espouses. His enthusiasm reminds me of a similar unleashing of joy coming from a British ultraorthodox Jew who in the 1990s was very much interested in my hopes for a renewed dynamic Jewish life in a reunited European continent after 1989. When I asked him why he was so interested in postcommunist developments, he replied in a most direct and surprising manner that for him the fall of the Berlin Wall had hastened the arrival of messianic times. (Would he still think so today?)

Beyond any messianic overtones, most Israeli policy institutes today favor a new reading of the Jewish world. Jews are no longer expected to make *aaliyah* (the ascent toward Israel, originally evoking the biblical ascent toward Jerusalem during the major holy days of pilgrimage), thereby abandoning their alienated status in the Diaspora. I, as a Jew living outside Israel, am now asked to stay where I live in order to defend Israel's legitimacy in a planetary struggle that has no borders. All Jews are considered to be on the barricades, regardless of where they live, because Israel wants to delocalize its defenses and the new horizon on this front, my friend tells me, is China. No one in Israel seriously believes that China will ever come to Israel's aid in case of major problems, but as my friend tells me, the weight of the world has shifted toward the Asian power, and the number of Israeli researchers writing policy papers on China corroborates this shift in emphasis. Interest in Europe, on the other hand, always according to him, is waning; researchers handle it more out of habit than true interest, except in terms of *that past.*

I think back to another epoch when other Jews reached the same conclusion that the weight of the world was shifting. It was 802 CE in Baghdad when Caliph Harun al-Rachid sent a delegation to Charlemagne's court in Aix-la-Chapelle, bearing a precious white elephant as a gift. There were Jews in the caliph's delegation, and they opened the way for other Jews to leave Baghdad and settle in nascent North Western Europe, which was perceived as the new frontier, in what would subsequently become the flourishing medieval Ashkenazi Rhineland communities.[8]

My friend is now pointing to Jerusalem at our feet. "You see," he tells me, "we must face two problems at once: the ultrareligious Jews, on the one hand, and the Arabs on the other." His solution is as crystal clear as his Cartesian mind honed by engineering studies in an earlier life. To contain the ultrareligious, he tells me, one must build hotels. These huge buildings full of semidressed tourists engaging in scandalous behavior (by ultraorthodox standards) will effectively block any ultraorthodox real estate development. When I ask him why these "black" Jews could not just leapfrog over such hotels, he is categorical in his reply: "No, hotels really do the trick because it is much too complicated to build beyond them." I understand this much: the ultrareligious shun all contact with secular Jews or anyone who does not share their lifestyle; such hotels can only be anathema to them.

But I am still puzzled by my friend's analyses. Who are these ultrareligious Jews whom he, the *Shtreiml*-wearing highly observant Jew, speaks about with such detachment? Are they anti-Zionists who do not recognize the legitimacy of a Jewish state that has not come about through divine will at the end of the messianic times? Such Jews could only offend him, who is a religious Zionist with a far more open and tolerant approach to the others of the world, including secular Jews as well as Muslims. Am I privy to a quarrel between different Jewish orthodox denominations, if that is the term? And if so, is this quarrel over links with the others in the world? A mathematical metaphor comes to mind. If you constantly divide by two even the smallest distance separating you from any geometrical point, you will never reach your goal. These ultraorthodox differences can hang on one hair under a *kippah* or encompass an entire cultural universe. Either way, they cannot be transcended.

My friend is in a hurry. He must rush to his weekly lesson with a Kabbalah master, a "really great one," he tells me, choosing not to divulge his name. These subjects are far too serious for his identity to be revealed to a secular Jew, and a woman to boot. He tells me only that his teacher can fathom the meaning of the world in all of its multiple dimensions, well beyond daily events. I believe him. In Jerusalem "the meaning of the world" cannot be grasped by simply relying on the news, policy papers, or conventional historical research. The city is a vast depository of underground tunnels, both literally and figuratively. As a result, they exert a very real pressure on the daily life of the country. Kabbalists in such a context are de rigueur.

It is surely with such complex references in mind that my friend points in the direction of the security fence on the horizon. He tells me that it has worked in containing the other danger: the Arabs. I look at him in an incredulous manner, pointing to East Jerusalem at our feet. With an optimism that combines his theological faith with his engineering background, he explains to me that Israel's policy of encircling the Arab quarters with new Jewish neighborhoods is beginning to yield its fruits. Sooner or later the Palestinian Arabs who are stuck inside the security barrier will want to join their fellow Palestinians in their lands on the other side. And he adds: "You know, there are many positive things going on in Ramallah today. This time they are really moving along in their state-building. They even have computers and all the attendant modernity. They too are beginning to have start-ups, and soon the vibrant new forces of the Palestinian nation will want to rally around Ramallah as the epicenter of their state."

I do not know how to react to such political optimism. My friend masters all the technologies of the twenty-first century, but (for the time being) he makes sure that his own eight children have no access to the Internet, or television for that matter. Yet he is confident that a few high-tech start-ups can help forge a Palestinian state.[9] *Start-Up Nation* is the title of an American best-seller that described Israel's economic miracle based on start-ups and high tech.[10] But transposed to a future Palestine, such a term takes on entirely different connotations. The Palestinian start-up has to be created from scratch: with Hobbesian state power (which Israel will most probably not allow), the rule of law, a viable political representation, social cohesion, and last but not least, an airport. Will it carry Arafat's name? Whatever the future may hold, even the fastest Internet broadband speeds cannot accelerate political and social time, even if regional harmony were to reign. But that is hardly the case.

My friend is the one who first used the term "psycho-rigidity" to describe ultrareligious Jews, when he explained to me years ago why he could not shake my hand. Now I am the one who is struck by his autistic optimism. Has he ever asked himself whether the Palestinians in question were really keen on moving to Ramallah? Since he personally would never contemplate the use of force against them, I have no idea which higher authority he could invoke to make them move. I know from previous conversations that one should not ask him to choose between the democratic agora and the burning bush: his mind is made up and it does not lean toward the Greek tradition. In the Kabbalistic world order, politics must occupy a very inferior and marginal sphere. But my friend does believe in the beauty of dialogue and in the importance of pragmatism. In his mind, the Arab residents of East Jerusalem will move out because, as perfect disciples of John Stuart Mill, it will be in their self-interest to do so. I admire his frankness because he says out loud what many Israelis silently wish for.

Other Israelis think otherwise. According to them, the Palestinians of East Jerusalem are choosing to take Israeli citizenship in ever-growing numbers, the best proof that they do not believe in a two-state solution.[11] But these Israelis who think in terms of a binational state may also be under an illusion. Palestinian residents of East Jerusalem who choose to become Israeli citizens do not necessarily adhere to any idealized political vision of joint peaceful coexistence. What they want above all is the right to keep their residence in East Jerusalem if they leave the city, the right to enlarge or to rebuild their houses without having to obtain a permit from the city authorities, a permit that is almost always denied, and above all a legal status that will allow them to fight off the growing number of ultraorthodox Jews who seek to take over or, as they say, to "reappropriate" houses in East Jerusalem.

As I contemplate the dry and empty hills on the other side of the separation wall, the hills where Palestinians should be building their start-up nation, I am reminded of Dino Buzzati's classic, *The Tartar Steppe*.[12] Buzzati's Italian novel was an existential meditation on an officer in a fort who spends his entire life waiting in utter boredom for the arrival of the Tartar enemy, and when the enemy finally arrives, is too old and sick to confront him. In reality the Israeli army controls most of these empty hills, and I am afraid that the Israelis will be confronting Palestinian "Tartars" in reverse. The latter will simply not cross over to the other side, or will do so only when Israelis will be too weak to impose it on them.

I do not pursue the metaphor. Could it be that I am simply stuck in my own petit bourgeois Western space/time? East Talpiot is there to remind me of other ancient worlds that constantly resurface in what is Israel's ever-changing temporal kaleidoscope. I am standing on the hill that dominates not only Jerusalem but the horizon all the way to the Dead Sea. This is the hill on which the Temple's high priest had his house. Christian tradition holds that it was in High Priest Caiaphas's house that the decision was taken to consign Jesus to the Roman authorities. This is probably why the hill was given the name "The Hill of Evil Counsel." This also happens to be the title of a novel by Amos Oz, a novel that conveys Jewish hopes and fears on the eve of the birth of the State of Israel.[13] And naturally, given Israel's multilayered kaleidoscope, this is also the hill where the British High Commissioner to Palestine had his own sumptuous palace built in 1933. Palestinian elites of all stripes, Jewish as well as Arab, were invited to attend elegant receptions and garden parties in a mansion that seemed destined to perpetuate British control over Palestine for generations to come. Barely fifteen years later, in 1948, the British left the palace to the Red Cross, which was responsible for taking care of the wounded on both sides of the Jordanian-Israeli War. With the armistice of 1949, the Red Cross turned the palace over to the United Nations, which still occupies it today. The palace served as the headquarters for the UN troops that were once stationed in the Sinai, and now serves for those that are stationed today on the Golan Heights and above all on the Lebanese border.

I learned all of the above thanks to an article in *Haaretz* in 2006. It was written by Danny Rubenstein, a journalist who, as a young soldier in the 1967 war, belonged to the unit that penetrated into the palace (then on the Jordanian side) and placed it under Israeli control.[14] The occasion for his article so many years later was the adding of three names on the commemorative plaque in front of the palace: the names of three UN soldiers who had just been killed by Israeli fire in the Lebanese War of 2006. The original first name on the plaque was that of Fokke Bernadotte, the UN representative who was killed by an Israeli terrorist attack in 1948. This was the same Bernadotte who had organized the "white bus" transport of Auschwitz survivors to Sweden in 1945. Descendants of those survivors now form the core of the Swedish Jewish community. *Déjà vu* all over again, Rubinstein seems to be saying. As a left-wing journalist he referred to Israel as an "apartheid state" in 2007 and was promptly disinvited from speaking at a meeting of the British Zionist Federation. When asked to make public apologies, he refused to recant, claiming that the term was banal and frequently used inside the *Haaretz* newsroom.[15] While reading about this skirmish I think of India, which has chosen to sell itself to the world with an ad campaign as "Incredible India." Israel should do the same, but under the title "Paradoxical Israel," for its own citizens are the harshest and most efficient critics of the state.

But let us return to East Talpiot, for the Hill of Evil Counsel has its own historical pendant, which could be called the ultimate place of Western nonmemory. It was in East Talpiot in 1980, during the construction of a new building, that workers found a stone mausoleum containing an ossuary on which were written the names of Jesus's entire family, including his own as the "son of Joseph." News of the excavation was made public only in 1996, surely because the nature of the findings was potentially explosive, particularly with respect to the Christian theology of the empty tomb. Since then there have been nonstop clashes of opinion over the tomb and the ossuary. A film was made and even a scientific conference was held to elucidate the subject further.[16] But the controversy continues, centering on the statistical probability of having all the Jesus family names appear on one single ossuary, on whether the carved letters or the patina that covered them were more recent additions, to finally focus on the role played by an Israeli collector, Oded Golan, with respect to the media announcements.[17] Scientific experts, archeologists, the Israeli antiquities division, world media, Jewish and Christian experts of the period, have all paraded at one time or another in front of Israeli courts in what is destined to remain a murky and perhaps unsolvable issue at the very heart of Jewish–Christian relations in the Western world.

One can easily understand why Jews and Christians would rather forget this controversial place of memory and let matters be. The former would rather not open useless polemics with their younger Christian brothers. The latter would rather not have to confront a historical challenge to their theological interpretations. Only the Muslims could take the Talpiot tomb in stride as a place of memory, because Islam recognizes Jesus as a prophet. But there are no longer any Arab Muslims left in East Talpiot. Besides, the tomb is apparently sealed off and inaccessible to visitors.

By 1972 the new neighborhood of East Talpiot where the tomb was discovered had been turned into a modern Jerusalem residential district for Israelis, built up as one of the very first Jewish settlements outside the Green Line, to the point that no one seems to remember that it once lay on the other side before 1967. More than a decade ago, I had gone to visit an elderly scholar who was a specialist of Jewish life in Eastern Europe before the Holocaust. Born in Poland well before the war, he was a very religious man and lived with his wife in a small, spartan apartment in East Talpiot. I had asked him upon arriving whether the "East" in "East Talpiot" meant that he was living on the other side of the Green Line. I can still remember his look of surprise at my question. After a long silence he replied, "I suppose so," with exactly the same tone in his voice of someone living in New York City or around Macôn in France being asked whether his house was situated on land that had once belonged to the Indians or Vercingetorix's tribe.

The biblical past in Jerusalem is visibly more pertinent and controversial than the most recent postwar past. With East Talpiot as an example, then, the new Jewish settlements around Jerusalem can simply go about blotting out the Arab past. My friend is convinced that Jewish urban pressure will win the upper hand over the Palestinian Arabs and their desire to remain inside the separation wall. So I am not surprised when he tells me: "We must hang on for two or three generations longer, after which *they* will understand that we are here to stay." But I tell myself that the Arabs who are taking Israeli citizenship surely have the same idea in mind. They too intend to "hang on": Trojan horses for a Trojan War that may or may not take place?

And almost as if he had read my thoughts, my interlocutor has already begun his own self-criticism. For one must always factor in the uncanny ability of most Israelis to juggle with what others would simply consider a schizophrenic pluralist language and outlook. He then begins to present his own doubts: yes, the Israelis were able to successfully encircle the Arabs of Jerusalem, but then he adds, with an ironic twinkle in his eyes, that nothing can prevent the same Arabs from encircling the Israelis. Before concluding: "We are engaged in a massive life-size game of Go."

The previous week, Bashir el Assad, Syria's embattled president, probably trying to get the spotlight off of his own crimes, had just unleashed a group of young Palestinians who rushed, unarmed, toward the barbed wire border on the Golan. The Israeli army, caught by surprise, fired at the surging crowd, killing several demonstrators. The secret nightmare of all Israelis and a new playing level in the life-size game of Go had just begun.

Suddenly, as we left East Talpiot, we were back inside an Israel that deeply wanted to move elsewhere. The man who is at once ultraorthodox but also exceptionally tolerant toward all others (while ensuring that his children lead strictly observant lives), an engineer and a Talmudist, a policy analyst and a Kabbalist, can think of his country's future, both in hope and in fear, not through the holy texts that he reveres, but only in terms of a strategic game from China.

4

IN THE EYE OF THE STORM

The man is seated behind the counter of his pottery shop reading a newspaper. There is not a customer in sight. He welcomes us with open arms, for he knows the British Jewish friend with whom I have come. She has been buying his pottery for many years for her secondary residence a few minutes away by foot in Mishkenot Sha'ananim, the first village founded outside the city walls by Moses Montefiore in the 1860s. We are inside the Armenian Quarter of the Old City, and the man is the heir to one of the most important pottery companies of Jerusalem, whose old kilns still are to be found behind his shop. He sells beautiful works of art with delicate geometrical and floral motifs painted in colors that are both subtle and luminous. But there are no customers.

The street and the little square where his shop is located are empty. He explains that this is all the fault of the municipal authorities, and he does so with a philosophical gesture of resignation behind which one can still feel all the anger. The mayor has changed all the signs at the Jaffa Gate so that they direct tourists straight to the Kotel, the Hebrew term for the Wailing Wall, where Jews gather to pray at the foot of the Temple Mount. As a result, our shopkeeper tells us, no one walks by his little square anymore, for it is not on the way. He shakes his head and adds: "Even the Armenians!" There is not a trace of historical revisionism in this sweet and calm man with beautiful light-green eyes and a trimmed mustache. Unlike many Muslims, he does not deny the historical existence of the Jewish Temple on the Mount. He is melancholic and resigned to the new order of things in a city whose historical contours are changing rapidly. To adapt, his family has opened another boutique on the other side of the Christian Quarter.

I listen to him with great interest. Just two hours earlier I had been given my "lesson from East Talpiot," and I realize that the nice Armenian constitutes the collateral damage of a project intended above all to marginalize the Arabs in the Old City. I think back to Teddy Kollek, the first mayor of reunited Jerusalem after the 1967 war, who was a much admired personality around the world. In June 2011, the 100th anniversary of his birth was celebrated with an exhibit inside Mishkenot Sha'ananim's cultural center, financed in part by the German Konrad Adenauer Foundation, which uses the center for its conferences. Inside the exhibit hall, Teddy Kollek's charismatic personality is evoked in several dozen paintings, the work of artists from around the world who flocked to united Jerusalem during his tenure, seeing in it the city of hope with peace around the corner. Would Teddy have changed the street signs? I doubt it. He was an ardent believer in his city's multicultural and multireligious component and would not have created express itineraries just to the Kotel. He considered it too great a privilege to get lost in the old streets and passages of the Old City, which had been off-limits to Israelis for nearly twenty years, to want to turn it into a one-track town.

We leave the shopkeeper and walk past the walls of the grand Armenian monastery, by the door of a small Armenian museum where a sign announces that it is closed for restoration. The sign is quite old and in several decades of walks in the Old City, I have never seen this small museum open. Next to it one can see pasted on the walls posters that evoke the Armenian genocide (a term the Turkish state has never accepted) in the Ottoman

Empire, with a map depicting the areas of the heaviest murders and the numbers involved. The maps are old and the colors they use to depict the different Armenian areas where the genocide took place are so faded that it is impossible to distinguish anything. Oblivion, despite the numerous European parliaments that have voted on behalf of the term "genocide" to qualify the Armenian massacres, triumphs over all else. It is as though the bitter memories of Armenian suffering had lost their edge compared to the far stronger and more recent memories of pain that this holy (far too holy) city has come to epitomize.

The silence in the Armenian Quarter contrasts powerfully with the noise and confusion in the adjacent Jewish neighborhood, particularly on the eve of Jerusalem Day. Jerusalem's center at the foot of the Old City is inundated with large tourist buses that have brought high school students from all over the country (and not just from the settlements on the other side of the Green Line) so that they can celebrate on the spot the anniversary of the city's reunification. Each student group, wearing T-shirts and caps with their school colors, walks behind a leader who carries an Israeli flag. In front of such a human wave, the center of the city, the new Mamilla shopping center, the Jaffa Gate and the Jewish Quarter of the Old City, all chockfull of youths, give the impression, seen from the air, of a vast Seurat-like pointillist painting. The only missing color is black, for the ultraorthodox youth are visibly absent from the celebrations. The years 1948 and 1967, Israel's key dates, are not important for them. They count their presence here in terms of millennia, or since the eighteenth century when Eastern European Jews returned significantly to the Old City. The students who throng to the city thus represent a new Israel that is at once secular and religious, young, and patriotic, and above all proud. They walk in the Old City as if they owned it . . . but as owners who look down on their non-Jewish tenants from another epoch who are still renting in their buildings. The pedigree, origins, and behavior of these tenants have now become factors in their eventual eviction. For these new young Israelis, the ultrareligious Jews, despite their differences, are integral members of this new national unity. They display it perhaps differently, but just as intensely.

The Jewish Quarter is in a frenzy of preparations for the big Jerusalem Day celebration that will take place in the evening in those very streets. Thick electrical cables are everywhere, leading to huge loudspeakers, plugged into the most sophisticated electrical consoles, worthy of top-notch rock concerts. The cafés on the path leading to the Kotel display impressive mounds of fast-food pizzas and falafels next to piles of canned soft drinks. The times when giants such as Coca-Cola and Pepsi did not have branches in Israel for fear of being boycotted in the Arab world are long gone.[1] All along the pedestrian path, above the old Roman Cardo (the axis that cut through the Old City) and the ancient portions that have been re-excavated, bakeries rival with one another to display the most tempting cakes from the Ashkenazi and Sephardic traditions: poppy, apples, and white cheese for the former; honey, almonds, and pine nuts for the latter. Even at the Jewish level, there is no intermingling of cultures. Each baker stands by his own tradition.

The houses that surround this main concourse are all new. They have been rebuilt and refurbished to serve as synagogues and Yeshivas in a quarter that was off-limits to the Jews between 1948 and 1967. Looking at the buildings, it is difficult to imagine just how biblically ancient this site is. The old Jewish Quarter has a virtual quality to it, as if it were its own hologram, on a site that seems far too modern to convey historical depth.

This quarter did not become modern by Jewish or Israeli design or because of any affinity with the modern style. It had to be entirely rebuilt after 1967. At the end of the 1948 war, the

Jordanian army and the Old City's Arab residents immediately and deliberately destroyed all Jewish traces, including small prayer halls dating back at least to the thirteenth century and the Crusades. The Israeli army having been proven unable to hold the Jewish Quarter, all the Jews who lived there had to be evacuated. The Old City thus remained without Jews for the first time in nearly a millennium, until the victory of 1967. The newness of the Quarter today thus symbolizes history's revenge with a return of Jewish life where it had been deliberately banned. The most important symbol of this return is the large, newly rebuilt Hurva Synagogue ("Hurva" means destruction in Hebrew), which was inaugurated in 2010. The one that was dynamited by the Jordanian army had been built in 1864 on the site of an older one that had been built in the early eighteenth century by highly orthodox Jews from Vilna and destroyed by Arab creditors over unpaid debts in 1721.

It is difficult not to be moved in front of this old/new presence. The Hurva Synagogue is still a bit too shiny white even in this refurbished quarter, but its pedigree is uncontested. It stands on re-excavated Jewish ruins dating back to the Second Temple. I am reminded of another rebuilt symbol, one that is less ancient in terms of historical and theological depth. By chance, I was in Dresden shortly after the newly rebuilt Frauenkirche was reinaugurated. Its beautiful white dome had been the centerpiece of Bellotto's classical eighteenth-century views of the city by the Elbe. The rebuilt church thus restored the city's skyline to its original beauty after the city was bombed massively by the British in 1943 and nearly destroyed. There too, one was confronted by the same exceedingly white hue of the stones, the same emotion of seeing a symbol reborn beyond the horrors of war, a carefully planned horror designed to sap the morale of the German people. . . . But here the difference with the Hurva is crucial: the Allies who bombed Dresden were not bent on destroying all traces of a German presence or even their physical existence on the spot. Both in Jerusalem and in Dresden time will play its role, and several decades from now the new stones will have acquired the semblance of the old, not unlike the rebuilt buildings near the Royal Palace in Warsaw, which have taken on an aged patina.

In Jerusalem, nothing is simple, however. The Old City possesses once again its three cupolas: The Dome of the Rock for the Muslims, the Saint Sepulchre for the Christians, and the Hurva for the Jews. In the more open societies of the Western world, the return of the third cupola would have been welcomed by those who worshipped in the other two, with visiting delegations and good wishes in an interfaith spirit. But this is Jerusalem: the site where the tectonic plates of the three monotheisms are on a permanent collision course. The "others" did not welcome with joy the return of the first monotheism on these holy sites. For the Muslims, the rebuilding of the Jewish Quarter and of the Hurva was perceived as one more humiliation inside an Old City that they consider entirely theirs and therefore part of future Palestine. The same is true for the Christian world as a whole, for only the Catholic Church has reformulated its theology vis-à-vis the Jews to the point of having Pope John Paul II pray at the Wailing Wall and even follow Jewish ritual by inserting a written prayer in its cracks. The Orthodox Christians who abound in the city have made no similar interfaith breakthrough. The Catholic transformation took time and was not always easy, and no one really knows if it might not change in a more distant future . . . changing for reasons that may be linked as much to Israel's own behavior in these neuralgic streets and alleys as to any possible resurfacing of the old Christian anti-Judaism. The city is a treasure trove of lessons in modesty for all of those who seek to appropriate it and interpret it in function of their own theology. Alas, no one in Jerusalem—past or present—however, has ever learned from the lessons of the past, seized as they are by the fever of certainty that seems to prevail in this transcendental spot.

During the writing of this chapter, I happened to be reading from a book I found in a Normandy flea market, with a very timely French title, *Terre promise et Palestine moderne,* "The Promised Land and Modern Palestine." Its author, a Hector Hoornaert, was a Belgian canon from Bruges and in his book he describes (in French, the only language of culture in Belgium at the time) his pilgrimage to the Holy Land with a group of French-speaking pilgrims during Easter week of 1912. Exactly 100 years have elapsed, and I am the very first person to be reading this particular copy of the book, since I have to cut open the still-bound pages. The noise they make under the pressure of the paper-cutting knife, is comparable to the sounds of a little boat's oars as they plunge in a tranquil river. There is something eternal and reassuring in this rhythmic sound and it adds a precious dimension to my own reflections.

I cannot resist the temptation to quote some lines from the good canon's book with respect to the Jews he encountered in the Old City. He too, like me, reached the Jewish Quarter from the Armenian side:

> One sees them in the streets, bogged down by their heavy garments, often with that classic fleeing look of a suspicious Pharisee. In the West, they are the flotsam and jetsam which revamped societies cannot absorb; here their mission is to represent faithfully their God-killing ancestors. In this fallen city, they are the consummate incarnation of decay, and this does not prevent them from swarming in their miserable quarter, where the opprobrium of the Muslims has confined them.[2]

This is the historical background against which one can measure the strength that inhabits all the young high school students as they parade through the Old City with their colored T-shirts, all the vigilant soldiers and policemen who patrol the streets, the ultraorthodox men who go about their daily lives in these streets, often accompanied by their very young wives with a cohort of children, women who, by excessive religious scruple, even wear a scarf over their wigs. Israel's determination and its autistic single-mindedness are also responses to this deeply antisemitic gaze.

Israel today, despite its claims of Zionist rebirth, remains the haunted child of these descriptions. Two centuries of Jewish emancipation in Europe, not to mention the Holocaust, constitute little more than the batting of an eyelid in Israel's plurimillennial pedigree. A question continues to haunt me. Is Israel today in the grip of youthful exuberance, an adult's hubris, or the blindness of old age? In the square where the Hurva Synagogue now stands, one feels all three at once. The rest of the world simply seems to have disappeared. Israel, much to my worry, celebrates itself with frightening insouciance.

A bit farther down the road, and we reach the steps that lead down to the Kotel. The crowd is increasingly dense and the music spots ever louder: every technician seems to be testing his own speakers in a cacophony that takes on symbolic connotations. Below, one can see the esplanade in front of the Wailing Wall, which is jam-packed with people. I have no desire to go down. With my British friend, I stop in front of the charity box that an ultrareligious Jew has placed strategically at the top of the steps. He is asking for contributions so that youths of his ilk can devote their lives to studying the Torah. Donors will receive one of those red string bracelets supposedly endowed with Kabbalistic virtues, which Madonna (the American) turned into a fashion icon.

We have just left an Israel celebrating somewhat ethnocentrically its victory over a very long diasporic past. I have no desire to enter a medieval court of miracles whose closest equivalent is to be found in Pushkar at the heart of India's Rajasthan. Push-kar, the holy city entirely devoted to the worship of Brahma, became one of the very favorite spots of international hippie culture in the 1970s. It has now become a compulsory stop for all those young Israelis who seek to forget their own country after their military service. In the Jewish world, there is an entire industry to try to bring back to Judaism these young Israeli Jews who are seduced by Asian spirituality in all its versions. The Lubavitch rabbi and his wife who were brutally murdered during the Mumbai terrorist attacks in November 2008 were in the city to offer a Jewish presence for all the traveling secular Jews and Israelis in the region. There are so many wandering about in India's cities that in Pushkar most stores and restaurants carry signs in Hebrew . . . and from afar the Hebrew letters bear an uncanny resemblance to their Sanskrit equivalents, albeit in a more rigid and angular version, as if the latter had all of a sudden developed tetanus, thereby losing their curves. In this city of pilgrimage, the old temples of Hindi veneration were all destroyed by the invading Muslim Moguls, who followed the strictest variety of Islam. The Hindi temples were rebuilt in the nineteenth century only after the decline of the Mogul Empire, just in time for the arrival of yet another, the British Empire, the same that governed Palestine under international mandate after World War I.

We thus head back once again through the Armenian Quarter and pass by the potter's shop. He is still there, reading his newspaper and still alone. As we leave the Jaffa Gate we are surrounded by an ever thicker crowd of young people. They are everywhere, even inside the gardens of the elegant King David Hotel. They sit in silence on the grass listening attentively to their professors, who must be explaining Jerusalem's long history and the ultimately very recent and final (to them) Jewish victory. I think back to an earlier scene I had witnessed while being driven by my ultraorthodox friend to East Talpiot. In the crowd of youths carrying Israeli flags, one strange flag stood out, carried by a young man in the middle of his burgundy T-shirt high school group. It was the invented flag of a possible future binational Israeli-Palestinian state, but with the Palestinian colors in predominance. The young man was brandishing this homemade flag with a certain vigor and it floated provocatively in the air: a Palestinian flag to which had been added at the bottom large white and blue stripes, as though someone had cut out part of a Greek flag to create it. Was this a crazy pastiche or an idealist statement? I assumed it was simply an act of rebellion on the part of a teenager who was sick and tired of being forced to prove his Israeli patriotism in a school cortege and felt like challenging his entourage. My friend, instead, chose to interpret this flag differently. He reached the conclusion that the young man was probably a Druze coming from a Druze high school in the north of the country. In his eyes, Israelis were forever privy to the danger of having the "others" in their midst. Suddenly the tidal wave of Israeli flags, the noise booming out of the loudspeakers in the Old City—the entire orchestration of such a patriotic day—appear terribly fragile.

These impressions of the Old City were reinforced three weeks later during a second trip to Israel. The setting, the second time around, was much calmer. The high school crowds with their patriotic purpose were gone, replaced by tourists. I returned to the Armenian Quarter to see whether the solitude of the potter had been simply linked to Jerusalem Day. Three weeks later, I find him still sitting alone with his newspaper, with very few people in the street. The esplanade in front of the Hurva Synagogue is full of tourists surrounded by the same ultraorthodox couples with their many children who go about their business totally indifferent to all those who do not fit their life style . . . as if a glass wall protected them.

A few steps beyond the square, I witness a very touching scene. On the steps of one of the many Talmudic schools, twenty fourteen- or fifteen-year-old students, dressed in the standard black-and-white outfits and bedecked with large black hats, are sitting on the steps with their teacher in the middle, all ostensibly supervised by an older man with a flowing white beard, who must be the school principal. They are having their end-of-year class picture taken. Will they spend the rest of their lives inside Yeshiva walls? Venturing outside only to stand on the steps leading to the Kotel to ask for money? Or will they be forced by the pressure of Israeli political equilibriums to submit to military service as the Tal Law that exempted them from military service comes up for reconsideration? Nothing is clear in this murkiest of murky areas of Israeli politics.[3] Two ultraorthodox men are on duty at the top of the stairs with their basket full of red bracelets, and they are doing quite a good job of grabbing potential donors. American Jewish tourists, visibly moved by the sight of men whom they deem to be the pious equivalents of their own Eastern European ancestors, give willingly and visibly.

This time around, I clear the basket of red bracelets and head down toward the Kotel. A few steps down I stop in a little square where groups of tourists are eagerly taking pictures. The Wailing Wall below is not the centerpiece of their photos. The tourists are busy taking snapshots of a large glass cube that contains a resplendent seven-branch menorah made of pure gold. The menorah is meant to be a copy of the one that stood in all glory at the center of the Second Temple—the same menorah that accompanied the Jewish prisoners to Rome after the destruction of the Second Temple and that was immortalized in the frieze of the Arch of Titus in the Roman Forum. A text near the menorah explains that it has been crafted to resemble the original as closely as possible in terms of size, gold alloy, and weight, according to the descriptions left by Maimonides, the great medieval Talmudist scholar. The final lines of explanation reveal the true purpose of the entire enterprise. The menorah is "worthy of being lit in the future Temple." And the text ends with: "May it (the Temple) be rebuilt speedily and in our time."

We have entered the realm of collective psychosis, for the reconstruction of the Temple can only take place if the Dome of the Rock, built on top of the Temple Mount by an Islam that appropriated for itself the previous holy site, is totally destroyed. There can be no real estate compromise.

The menorah belongs to the Temple Institute, a nongovernmental organization created in 1987 by non-Haredi ultranationalist religious Zionists with one purpose in mind: to reclaim the Temple Mount from the Muslims, to rebuild the Temple destroyed by the Romans, and to resume the old pre-rabbinical Hebrew rituals with their animal sacrifices. To fulfill its mission, the Institute is engaged in a wide range of activities, which are all explained on its website, www.templeinstitute.org. It is important to visit it. It tells us the institute's members are busily preparing for the ancient rituals that ended when the Romans destroyed the Temple in 70 CE, and this implies, of course, preparing for a new caste of priests. The Institute's workshops have already reproduced the ceremonial outfits the priests will wear, including the outfit of the Great Priest with its breastplate of twelve precious stones, one for each tribe of Israel. They have already created the golden altar where the incense will be burned as well as the table (made of gilded wood) where bread is to be presented. The bronze ladle used for the hand washing ritual, we are told, is still being designed. All of these copies, ready for operational use, are on display in the Institute's museum, where one can also find a large collection of oil paintings depicting the Temple from all sides. The website specifies that the paintings are the work of former Soviet Jews who upon arriving in Israel painted them as a way of coming closer to the religion of their forefathers. Clones of Andreï Rublev in a twenty-first-century Jewish version of the great fifteenth-century master's icons? The aesthetic qualities of these paintings invalidate any such comparison.

The only missing element (for the time being) that is holding up the rebuilding effort is the perfectly red heifer, whose birth will signal the beginning of the messianic times, for its ashes were vital during the Temple Period for the purification rituals of the priests.[4] Upon learning this bit of news, I suddenly remember having read somewhere that those who adhere to this movement are not the kind to sit around patiently waiting for these times to arrive. They are actively using the most advanced genetic techniques in order to facilitate the breeding of such a red heifer in Israel's own agricultural laboratories. The Möbius strip thus unites the most archaic Judaism with the most advanced Israeli technology.

The Institute clearly draws its largest support and most of its activists from the American Jewish world with its powerful *self-help* ethic. The whole project is presented with such an American spin. The menorah, the priestly garments, the ritual objects are all referred to literally with the words Neil Armstrong used when he became the first man to walk on the moon: "a small step for man and a giant leap for mankind." The institute's ultimate message: one should not wait passively for the messianic times, but must actively provoke their coming.

This is no fringe movement. Its adepts all militate on behalf of the Greater Israel that would occupy the entire West Bank, and they are remarkably efficient in conveying their ideology. One has to watch the three videos they have produced for their

"Temple Esplanade Tour" under the guidance of one of their rabbis, and, as they assert, "while scrupulously observing the Halakhic prescriptions of not treading on the Temple's Holy sites." The tour starts out with a historic review that "justifies" future hope in the messianic times, but it does not take long for it to turn into a lambasting of the current Israeli state for not having the courage to kick the Muslims out of the Temple Mount . . . and out of Israel. The arguments used in the video are deliberately very rational and convincing in their own way: very difficult to rebut. Besides, the Muslim authorities over the Temple Mount are there to give them credence by their own behavior and by their desire to destroy all traces of a previous Jewish past: by throwing away biblical rubble, brought to the surface when they built an underground mosque, thus reinforcing the generally widely shared Muslim tenet that the Temple never existed. The Jewish militants also underscore another very simple fact: the Temple was the *only* holy Jewish site on earth, whereas by praying toward Mecca, the Muslims clearly acknowledge that the Dome of the Rock is a secondary religious shrine. Therefore, in these Jewish eyes, priority should be given to the Jews, the first and the only legitimate owners. It is difficult to challenge a group whose self-proclaimed purpose is to "restore God's honor."

The menorah may be the property of an extremist private group. But unless proven otherwise, the place where it sits— next to the steps leading to the Kotel—is a public space. We have entered Israel's eye of the storm: the scene of extremely subtle balancing acts with extremely dangerous background noises. Israel, for the vast majority of its citizens, was not created in order to reestablish the Second Temple. But . . . the very same seven-armed menorah is the official symbol of the State of Israel, and significantly, the official car of the Israeli president has only the menorah as its license plate.[5] The Temple group may not recognize the legitimacy of the State of Israel, which it perceives as a "lay usurper which behaves like an ostrich in its fear of offending the Muslims."[6] But the state, on the other hand, cannot deny the group's legitimacy, if only because Israel has no official separation of synagogue and state, and a Jew, however extremist, still remains a Jew. As a result of this political-religious fuzziness, the group's exhortation to rebuild the Temple cannot be outlawed, and thousands of Jewish tourists swallow its message lock, stock, and barrel, deeply moved by this earnest desire to become once again absolute masters over Israel's holy past. The golden menorah in its glass case has to all effects and purposes become the vertical antechamber to the Wailing Wall.

The Wall: During this second trip I am finally willing to confront it. To describe the ambiance around the Kotel, I shall once again revert to the words of the pious canon a century ago, despite the fact that they are imbued with Christian theology's anti-Judaic prejudices of the time. I do so because his words offer a strange echo to the current thinking of most orthodox, conservative, and liberal Jews today who contest the taking over of the monumental (both in physical and in symbolic terms) site by an ultraorthodox coterie.

After having described the physical aspect of the Wailing Wall, which he discovered after emerging from a narrow labyrinth of alleys (these were destroyed by the Israeli army after the Six Day War, precisely to allow an easier access to the Wall), the nice canon has difficulty understanding what he sees before him. We are in 1912, the Jewish presence in Jerusalem is growing in what is commonly referred to as the "Yishuv" (the term used to define organized Zionist Jewish settlement in the last years of the Ottoman Empire and during the British Mandate). But the canon knows nothing about these early Zionists, and this explains his surprise upon seeing what he defines as "European" Jews on the spot:

They now carry out their cult (in front of the Wall) and turn to it, as though it were a silent divinity, to whom they offer the perpetual sacrifice of their sorrowful gestures and of their tears. It is a spectacle which one contemplates at first with stupor, without understanding any of it, since it is so unexpected.

And he continues:

Their clothing bears no connection to the miserable housing nearby; they have the decency to wear clothing which befits a religious moment. Shawls with colored stripes cover their outfits, and among the men wearing the caftan, one can spot many who wear European clothes.

Adding:

They consider the Wall to be a living Being; they kiss it with loving gestures as though carried away by a painful and timeless meditation going back to vanished centuries. Others, who are less passive, after having dried away their tears, bang their heads against the insensitive granite, as if to blame it for its inaction, while exhorting the accomplishment of the texts they proffer.

To conclude:

There is nothing feigned or inappropriate in their attitude. These Jews stubbornly attach their lives to the promises of Israel's prophets. For them the Letter has killed the Spirit: in our eyes they resemble condemned men who are trying to expiate their crimes.[7]

For the canon, given his Christian faith of one hundred years ago, the Jews are wrong of course. Israel's prophets had predicted Jesus's arrival as the Messiah, and in their guilty stubbornness the Jews refused to acknowledge him; they thus continue to pray in front of the Wall as though it were a silent divinity. The reference to Abraham's idols is obvious. And the canon finishes off with a perfectly Christian reflection, before the Catholic Church embarked in its post–Vatican II Copernican Revolution, reinforced by the Holocaust commemorations with respect to the Jews, now considered to be the Church's "elder brothers":

> This Wall is a human artifact and these Jews do not understand that what they ask of it has already been granted to humanity by the Calvary. There, above us, the otherworldly Kingdom opened, while here below, it is the Gehenna and divine justice pushes, against a vain idol, the criminal traitors toward their Savior. Stones have replaced Christ's heart.[8]

Remove from these quotes all Christian references and replace them with "Judaism's spiritual and ethical values" and you will have the gist of what leading enlightened Jewish philosophers, Talmudists, and rabbis, orthodox as well as conservative and liberal, preach today. All rise up against this worshipping of the Wailing Wall, which is not only a human artifact as the canon sustained, but moreover, as archeologists now believe, even a post-Herodian construction.[9] For the scholars of the Shalom Hartman Institute as well as for many philosophers such as Moshe Halbertal, who has played a leading role in the renewal of orthodox thought and was the co-author of the Israeli army's (IDF) code of ethics in war, Jewish ethics is endangered by these Jewish "idolaters." They venerate the old biblical lands at the expense of the well-being of the Jews and their Palestinian neighbors, thus renewing with the tradition of the golden calf.[10] In such a reading, the gold menorah in the glass display and the Temple Institute are little more than a golden calf without four legs. Israel's and the Jewish world's leading philosophical, legal, and historical experts all counter in their understanding of Judaism the old canon's accusations that the Jews only venerate "stones."

Nothing, however, is simple in Israel. The activists at the Temple Institute are also against the idolatry of the Wailing Wall. They don't want Jews to pray next to the Wall, which they consider as a poor substitute for the real thing. They want them to be able to engage in the glorious rituals that they had at the height of their glory when they prayed in the Temple on the Mount. To reinforce their credo, they have tacked onto the gates leading to the praying area of the Wall a set of rules that sound perfectly reasonable for any religious site: proper attire, no food, and the request to speak softly. But the reasons for this request are highly controversial because they seem to defy the entire Talmudic tradition. The Shekinah, the Hebrew term for the light that accompanies the divine presence, according to these guardians of the Temple (in the literal sense of the term), is still *inside* the Temple Mount. The Talmud instead, as the guidebook of the Jews in exile, had transformed this idea, valid until the destruction of the Second Temple, into a far deeper symbolical notion. The Shekinah thereafter was to be found wherever the Jewish people came together in collective prayer and was deemed to follow them throughout their peregrinations.

The implications of this rift are portentous. If the Shekinah is still trapped inside the Temple Mount, then it is the duty of the Jewish people to liberate it (just as in the fairy tales or in Mozart's operas) by surging forward against the Muslim presence. If the Shekinah accompanies instead the Jewish people wherever they may reside, then it can shine forth peacefully from inside the Green Line and even from within the Diaspora. Unfortunately, there is no way to solve these tensions through any rational or logical debate. Nor can they be calmed politically, given Israel's ambiguous definition as the Jewish state.

One has thus entered an entirely different space/time, one that is no longer cybernetic or even symbolical, but quite literally down to earth, an earth sanctified one stone at a time.

A metal detector and a screening machine separate the Jewish Quarter from the Muslim Quarter in the Old City. Significantly, it works only one way. The Palestinians cannot stop any Jew who might appear suspicious in their eyes. The numbers of such Jews never cease to grow, given the actions of a powerful movement bent on reclaiming old Jewish houses in the Muslim Quarter. Some of these houses do indeed bear Jewish inscriptions (such as stars of David) on their exterior stone walls, and may have served in the past (but how old a past?) as places of prayer or community rooms when all of Jerusalem fit into the Old City. But by walking in the narrow streets, one notices young ultraorthodox women with strollers coming out of houses that seem to contain no visible sign of previous Jewish life. They walk by, unperturbed by the silent gaze of their Arab neighbors, because they are convinced of the religious sanctity of their *reconquista*. They simply don't see the Arabs in whose midst they have settled, for in their eyes these men and women are just the latest incarnation of all those "others" who have always hated and who continue to hate Israel, the land and the people.

These streets have come to resemble an ancient arena where Israeli and Arab gladiators (the former extremists, the latter helped by Israeli human rights organizations) fight each other through opposing epochs and trajectories. We have entered another spatial and temporal dimension, one totally impermeable to the terrestrial diplomacy and geopolitical equilibriums of our time. The third presence in these contested streets is Christian. But the pilgrims who enter this arena in search of their own holy sites along the Via Dolorosa look like startled witnesses overwhelmed by the intensity of the struggle between the Abrahamic faiths' first and third child.

The combat of these ultraorthodox extremists is frightening, for it endangers Israel's future and that of the entire region, but it is not entirely incomprehensible. Who could have ever imagined that the Jewish people would settle again in their land of origin? That the Kotel would become, for better and worse, that place of spiritual encounter where even a pope would make a pilgrimage? That the danger that floats above the Jewish Quarter of the Old City is not decay and oblivion, as the canon seemed to think a century ago, but the blinding of a triumphant hubris? I return to the canon's words, not because of the intellectual depth of his thinking, but for the illusions he had concerning a Christian reconquest of the Holy Land. May they serve as a warning:

> The Christian armies of the Middle Ages for having relied far too much on human means, lost an ephemeral kingdom: nowadays, slowly but surely, love for Christ the Redeemer is building another.[11]

And the canon furnishes as proof the growing presence of religious orders throughout the Holy Land and their good works toward the local Arab populations, to conclude, this time, "Christ is reborn where he had died":

> Jerusalem has kept its old aspects, but its history had entered a new era. On its soil, new pacific Crusaders have established their camp; they do not want to take anything, from the city but to give it all they have, in the name of Christ, by offering the city true religious life and the civilization which accompanies it.[12]

This "new period" ended less than forty years later. Reading these lines, I remember the sight of an Italian Dominican priest, speaking sotto voce on his mobile phone, alone like a minuscule white dot in the midst of all the ultraorthodox Black Jews at the Kotel celebrating their victory over history and the triumph of their memory . . . but with on the other side of the metal detector an entire Arab Quarter laboring its own field of memory. Whoever meditates on the history of Jerusalem can only suspend judgment over any predictions concerning its future, for it runs on its own highly special time. For rosy futures, it is best to seek comfort in technology's prowess.

5

ROOTED UTOPIAS

One figure says it all. Israel has more companies listed on the NASDAQ, the high-tech stock market, than all of Europe. Everything else is only commentary.[1]

The kibbutz and the army were the two traditional pillars of historic Israel's scientific research establishment, founded by Zionist immigrants from Europe. Their very real but also symbolic weight still conditions the two major axes of Israel's scientific miracle: agricultural research and technological innovation linked to Israel's military and security needs. A third axis of high technology, however, incarnates the new Israel, the one that lives in its own cyberspace well beyond its old borders.

Official secular Israel has just produced its own existential "Pentateuch" (the five books that compose the Torah) to describe an Israeli scientific future worthy of the Garden of Eden. It is a white brochure, widely distributed during the 2011 President's Conference, and published by the Hebrew University of Jerusalem to present its faculty's scientific innovations and research, which are then commercialized by Yissum, the university's own technological transfer company. Each chapter of this brochure covers a different aspect of this scientific new world: nutrition and plant research, medical and health-related innovations, new technological tools, new security technology, and progress in the realm of sustainable growth.[2]

One can only remain dazzled by such a display of scientific creativity with global implications, whether it is in the agricultural realm on behalf of the poorest countries or in a lighter vein in order to bring back perfume and taste to our frequently insipid and standardized agro-industrial produce. The security realm, meanwhile, is moving into new, ever less aggressive directions, and new computer programs are transforming all disciplines, including the most ancient, be they archeological or literary.

Nevertheless, as I read on, these innovations, despite their impressive scientific qualities, take on an increasingly problematic aspect. The brochure is the display window Israel wishes to present to the world: despite all the dangers it must confront, this technological David still manages to rank among the very best in the world in terms of research. The brochure is worth examining in greater detail but with one caveat in mind: it proves, for better and worse, just how Israel lives and thinks of itself as being light-years away from its neighborhood, even—or especially— when it seeks to interact with it. In the end one is tempted to ask whether the country's scientific prowess isn't buttressing and even reinforcing the mediocrity of its political class: by offering policymakers palliative technical solutions with respect to the country's existential and political problems.

The scientific advances presented in the brochure all seem poised to solve humanity's problems, most often through genetic breakthroughs. How can one reduce obesity in our rich developed countries? By eating even fat and sugary food *at the right moment* in the chronobiological cycle when they can be absorbed usefully in the metabolic process. Do vegetables wilt on the supermarket shelves of the world? One can make them keep their fresh aspect far longer while also giving them added taste and savor and even greater beauty, *and* enabling them to grow on parched land with ever less water or even where there is only saline water available. Moral of the story: only man's folly prevents the Horn of Africa from feeding its own.

Are some important medicinal plants too rare or their active molecules too difficult or too expensive to extract, with the consequence that some vital medicines are too costly? No problem: one can isolate the medicinal properties of these molecules and inject their genes into easily accessible plants that grow far more quickly. As a result, the tobacco plant, itself responsible for one of humanity's gravest ills, has redeemed itself by hosting the genes of *Artemisia annua,* which provides effective treatment against malaria. The tobacco plant has now been turned into the equivalent of a small, constantly renewable pharmaceutical factory capable of growing where the medicine is most needed.

The introduction of Nile perch into Lake Victoria as a crazy commercial venture led to an ecological disaster when the fish that used to nourish the local populations were wiped out.[3] No problem. Israelis found a way of transferring their carp farm technology to Africa by creating more resistant breeds and developing appropriate ponds where the carp can live and grow without any external nutritional input. They then taught the local peasants how to master the carp life cycle . . . and as a result protein returned to the daily diet of Lake Victoria's populations. The brochure does not say whether they were also given the Eastern European Jewish recipes for gefilte fish . . .

The Jews, even during the worst moments of their diasporic life, were always given the right to study medicine. It is therefore no accident that they were often court doctors. Their competence was strengthened further by their social marginality, which guaranteed that they would not participate in any court cabals against the king. Israel inherited this long medical tradition and elevated it, thanks to its security and military needs, to the highest levels. Mini electric canes transmitting vibrations captured from the part of the brain that would normally have controlled vision now allow the blind to "see" the mass and height of objects that surround them. Nanorobots composed of proteins accelerating cell growth help avoid infections by healing large and deep wounds but also the smaller ones incurred by diabetics. New fluorescent molecules injected in the body identify and affix themselves to cancerous or arthritic cells that they then kill off without damaging the healthy cells nearby. New proteins can now inhibit brain sensors modified by drug addiction, thus fostering the hope of reducing the very high rates of relapse. Mathematical models allow researchers to better understand the evolution of bacteria when antibiotics are given, so as to better control their use. Finally, satellites can be programmed to follow patient movements before and after major operations to compare the results and quantify their effective daily progress.

The brochure's leitmotiv: everything can be better understood thanks to science. Biblical texts, ancient pottery shards, medieval documents, all "speak" more clearly since they have been scanned and digitized in ways that can reconstitute their original content, and even help unravel obscure meanings and shapes by proposing alternatives. Nanotechnologies can do the same by creating "human" microchips containing all the genetic information of the various human organs that can be used to generate "human" cells to be used in pharmaceutical and dermatological research. As a result, testing on animals is no longer necessary, all the more so that their physiological characteristics do not fully correspond to those of human beings. These microprocessors, furthermore, are faster and consume less energy than the older variety because they use green particles from the world of plants.

On the security front, Israeli researchers can now recognize in a crowd those individuals who have abnormally high stress levels, individuals who can therefore be intercepted in a nonviolent manner *well before* they can commit terrorist attacks or dangerous crimes. Similarly, researchers are learning how to read brain waves before they are translated into the physical re-actions that lead to verbal communication. Patients who can no longer express themselves in a conventional manner will thus be able to communicate differently with their entourage. And of course such discoveries will allow doctors to identify the nature of a coma and whether the patient still hears and can respond. All of these discoveries make one think back to Steven Spielberg's 2002 film *Minority Report,* which was based on the hero's ability to anticipate the future, with catastrophic consequences.

Similarly the brochure tells us that Israeli scientists are learning (albeit still in a rudimentary manner) to predict the onset of earthquakes and floods. Other research, perfected thanks to the needs of the military, has allowed specialists to figure out how to better protect the body through use of a microscopic analysis of a bullet's impact on different organs. Another new system can condense all the information in a twenty-four-hour surveillance video by displaying simultaneously every person or vehicle and identifying them by their characteristics and exact time of passage.

Nor has ecology been left behind. Agronomists are learning how to recycle vegetable waste into protein food for animals, such as olive pits for cattle, thanks to the acid-breaking proper-ties of a fungus. New biological components also allow for far smaller doses of pesticides to be used in fields, while ensuring that they do not contaminate the soil's deepest layers. Genetic manipulation now enables researchers to "shut off" the nefari-ous genes of insects, thus allowing them to gather nectar and pollen without mildewing or rotting the fruits and flowers they touch. Other microorganisms are now capable of stabilizing dunes to prevent further desertification. Ultrapowerful batter-ies can now run green cars, and a new green architecture based on solar and wind energy is transforming cities. Israel has been a world leader in mobile phone technology for decades, and its researchers are now implementing a fourth generation of phones whose 3-D applications will respond to a simple gesture of the hand.

This long list is far from exhaustive, and it concerns only research carried out at the Hebrew University of Jerusalem. For the sixtieth anniversary of the State of Israel, sixty scientific projects had been chosen through a national competition to exemplify the country's scientific vitality. Most projects had benefited from Israel's defense technology: drones that could find wounded soldiers in the field, and robots that could give them immediate medical attention where no doctor could go. Cameras that could see behind walls in order to better locate hostages or prisoners. Artificial arms and legs capable of accomplishing the most precise and refined movements, and the reconstruction of organs and the creation of new medicines whose efficiency was multiplied by the use of stem cells.

Israel, of course, is not the only country to engage in these types of research, but given its tiny size, it is the most productive, because it is a world leader in all of these fields. Several structural givens help explain Israel's position, and all of them incidentally facilitate the country's move into its own temporal space.

Contrary to countries with a Christian background, Israel has not had to face the least obstacle in its genetic research. Judaism thinks of man as God's assistant in the ongoing task of creation and considers it his duty on earth to carry it out (as conveyed in the concept of *Tikkun Olam*). The Jewish worldview thus facilitates and even encourages scientific innovation for the improvement of life. The ultraorthodox are very interested in scientific research, particularly genetic research, whose preventive breakthroughs allow them to intermarry while avoiding genetic diseases prevalent in their communities. At a more universal level, Israel's climate and its agricultural conditions have pushed the country to find appropriate scientific solutions that are also highly relevant for the poorest countries on earth. This type of research follows up on the tradition of the young (and poor) newly born state of Israel that at the onset thought of itself as belonging to the group of postcolonial nonaligned nations formed in the 1950s in Bandung (by countries such as India and Indonesia), before Israel was expelled from its ranks. Contrary to the needs of most advanced nations, one can say that what is good for Israel can also be good for developing countries because they all share the same physical constraints. Furthermore, Israel's African projects are imbued with the country's ethical focusing on the sanctity of life. This is not necessarily the case for China's projects in Africa, which are uniquely focused on China's own economic and cultural interests.

On the other hand, Israel, by turning toward the developing world or that of emerging societies, especially in non-Christian Asia, is not really coming any closer to its Arab or Muslim neighbors. Research on the consequences of desertification in its neighborhood reveal that the Israeli-Egyptian border is highly visible from satellite photos: the land on the Israeli side is dark and fertile, whereas the land on the Egyptian side is quite pale, stark proof that it has been overgrazed. There are even unintended moments of pure irony in the brochure's projects when one can read about transborder pollution in the Middle East in the following terms:

Previous studies indicated that 23% of the year, air masses arrive in Israel from Saudi Arabia, Jordan and North Africa, mainly during transitional seasons and often containing desert dust. For 66% of the time, air masses come from Western and Eastern Europe, the latter related to the synoptic situation of the low pressure Persian system, which exists in Israel for most of the summer months.[4]

And the researcher goes on to affirm that in the summer 50 to 70 percent of all particles emanating from aerosols found in Israel's atmosphere come from Eastern Europe. It is difficult not to read these phrases in a metaphorical manner. All the relevant geographic references for Israel's identity and fears are there: the country's East European origins, its North African migrations, and its biggest threat, the "Persian system," which in this case is not really "low pressure."

After I finished reading the impressive list of Israeli scientific achievements, I was seized by a metaphysical doubt. What if these achievements, rather than helping Israel, had instead aggravated its regional standing and even its position in the world? The problems Israel must solve are of a political and social nature. No scientific miracles can solve them, because they belong to an entirely different order where progress is measured in terms of humanistic willpower rather than technical feats.

One would be tempted to say that the country that created mini electrical canes so that the blind can "see" the mass and volume of objects before them should have produced a few more models of a geopolitical nature that would allow Israel to "see" the obstacles that surround it and that the country continues to ignore as if the Palestinians could continue to accept the status quo indefinitely. Fantastic robot cameras allow Israelis to localize hostages or terrorists even behind very thick walls? The same cameras might enable the religious extremists to one day see what hidden spaces still lie inside the Temple Mount, even if they may not find the trapped Shekinah inside according to the fundamentalists of the Temple Institute. But the same cameras do not allow Israelis to see the chaos that the building of the separation barrier created in the lives of Palestinian families whose villages were cut off from their lands, effectively making an entire people the hostages of its extremists (unless the construction was deliberately designed to push the villagers toward Ramallah).

One has the feeling that Israel in trying to separate itself from its neighbors has used them as so many vaulting poles with which to catapult itself into a peaceful because distant globalization. The army and the kibbutz. by historically protecting the country. In effect distanced it from its not so natural ecosystem. And the world of high technology has only worsened the situation.

The Matam high-tech park just outside Haifa could be literally anywhere in the world. Its buildings have the same neutral aspect of all modern business offices: functional, air conditioned, with internal security, surely endowed with their own generators in case of electric cutoffs, with built-in gyms, cafeterias, and open-space offices to facilitate creative dialogue, and, I imagine (for I have never been inside), the usual classic arsenal of green plants for ecological reasons—unless these have been replaced with cactuses since we are in Sabra-driven Israel (Sabra is "cactus" in Hebrew as well as the name of the first generations of Israeli-born citizens). "Silicon Wadi" in Israel, named after the American Silicon Valley, is not its ersatz or local franchise. This is where the new high-tech giants have set up their R&D divisions. The list of those companies that avail themselves of Israel's scientific talent is long: Google, Microsoft, Intel, IBM, Yahoo, Philips, Facebook, and many more soon to come. It would be simpler to list those companies that don't have offices in Matam, a center that was set up only five years ago. But in the world of high technology and its start-ups, five years is the equivalent of a century.

As further proof of Israel's decoupling from our own Western world, the Matam center was created in 2006 in the midst of Israel's second Lebanese war. At the time all foreign eyes were riveted on the conflict between Israel and the Hezbollah, with everyone wondering how far the Israeli army would penetrate inside Lebanon this time around, while also commenting that the damage caused to the Lebanese villages close to the border was quite disproportionate to the slowness and inconclusiveness of the tanks' progress. Everyone, both inside Israel and outside, seemed to agree that the Israeli army was no longer as brilliant and effective as in the past. Moreover, it was accused of using banned arms and chemicals in its warfare: phosphorous bombs and fragmenting bullets. Some voices from the old Israeli left claimed that the army was less efficient because its troops had been denatured by the police operations they had to undertake in the occupied territories. On the Israeli side, the attack had been provoked by the pounding of Israel's northern villages with ever more effective missiles in an ever widening perimeter of action, proof that Iran was arming the Hezbollah. The inhabitants of the Galilee were spending entire days in their shelters and their children had been evacuated farther south. Even Haifa seemed threatened.

I do not know whether this war changed Hezbollah's behavior or the military tactics of the Israeli army. However, it indirectly produced, almost by ricochet, three masterpieces—two films and a novel—all of which had the Lebanese war(s) in the plural as leitmotif. Avi Folman's *Waltz with Bashir* (2008), Samuel Maoz's *Lebanon* (2010), and David Grossman's novel *To the End of the Land,* whose English title does not fully evoke the pessimism of its Hebrew original, "A woman fleeing the announcement."

At the heart of Grossman's book lies the Lebanese war of 2006, a war that took the life of his officer son, Uri, and that Grossman had criticized from the very first day. This war (with the 1967 war and a love triangle in the background) is ever present in the novel, as the heroine, a soldier's mother, leaves her house so as not to be there should the army officers show up to announce that her son had been killed: her departure, in brief, is a way of conjuring fate. The two films instead evoke the experiences lived by simple soldiers during the 1982 Lebanese war. *Waltz with Bashir,* shot as a comic book strip, does so through a psychoanalytical account of anguished adult Israelis who cannot remember what they experienced in their units when they were stationed close to the Sabra and Chatila camp, the camp in Beirut where Palestinian refugees were murdered by Lebanese Christian militias while the Israeli army nearby took no action. The soldiers might not remember, but they all seem to have incorporated the horror of that moment into their recurring nightmares, and nearly three decades later they try to come to terms with that past. The film *Lebanon* offers instead one of the most powerful critiques of war, as seen by a mature man who looks back on his experiences as a new army recruit who was in the heat of the action during the first Lebanese war but could only capture limited snippets of it through the turret of his tank.

These three works of art each incarnate in their own way Israel's total decoupling from its neighbors, particularly when it wages war against them. In Grossman's novel, the entire action takes place in the head of the mother who rethinks all of her family life while she hikes toward Israel's northernmost border (thus right next to Lebanon) with the man who in reality is her son's biological father. The Israeli Arabs who live in the villages where the couple stops to buy food during their hike are as absent from the story as the enemy on the other side of the border. In this book, the Israeli pain is autistic.

This is all the more remarkable, given that David Grossman is surely the Israeli novelist who has written most about Arab suffering at the hands of Israelis. The circumstances of his latest

2012 foray are worth noting in detail. In a long op-ed piece in *Haaretz,* he reflects on the 2008 death by willful negligence and indifference of a Palestinian Arab petty thief from Gaza. The man had entered Israel illegally, stolen a car, and wounded himself in the subsequent car crash. Hospitalized, still under perfusion, he was turned over to the Israeli police, who when refused entrance at the Gaza checkpoints by the soldiers on duty, simply dumped the Palestinian by the wayside, in the middle of the night, like a dog, knowing that he would die. Their tour of duty had ended and they did not want to be burdened with this human cargo. Grossmann's reflection, considered by many as his *"J'Accuse"* against Israel's loss of moral conscience, was published in a most revealing manner. *Haaretz* chose exceptionally to place the op-ed piece on its front page in the Israeli edition, but refrained altogether from publishing it in its English world edition. Needless to say, a translation of the article into English appeared on the Internet almost instantly.[5] But while Grossmann's article provoked much soul-searching within a concerned Israeli public, most Israelis were not aware that the article had not been published in English and most foreigners were not aware that it had appeared at all.

In *Waltz with Bashir* the horror of Sabra and Chatila becomes the backdrop for a remarkable psychoanalytical study of forgetfulness, but neither the Lebanese nor the Palestinians who died during that war ever emerge as protagonists. The entire film is focused only on Israeli anguish. *Lebanon* is a masterpiece worthy of the great film classics on the nature of war. But it has one major flaw: its title. There is not the slightest trace of Lebanon in the film and even less so of the Lebanese populations who suffered and died during the war. One does see at one point two or three soldiers (one of whom is not even Lebanese but Syrian) who seem to play the role of bad Indians in an American Western. It came as no surprise that many Lebanese criticized both films and their directors for having used Lebanon as an abstract reference that allowed them to obtain what these critics called "a pardon through film" in a world where those who did the invading ended up winning the Golden Lion in Venice.[6] The film should have been called *Israel* because the metaphor of a world shrunk to what can be seen from the narrow perspective of a tank turret fits perfectly Israel's political context today.

The Matam high-tech park in Haifa instead incarnates Israel's wide-angle vision, a vision so ultramodern that neither geography nor borders seem to count any longer. Matam's interlocutors are global: they may live on the other side of the planet, but they are constantly available through videoconferencing and the Internet. It would be a mistake, however, to think of "tank turret" Israel and Matam Israel as antithetical. The two focal lengths are complementary. While the two films and the novel, with all of their autistic tragedy, were maturing in the minds of their creators in the wake of the Lebanon wars, other Israelis were going about their daily lives busy with their own material and technological preoccupations, while still others patiently labored at their biblical and Talmudic commentaries. In doing so they were not on a collision course but were in effect composing Israel's cubist man à la Picasso or Braque.

High technology has furnished the necessary perspective that gives depth of field and meaning to Israel's renaissance. The "start-up" revolution has in effect replaced the kibbutz of the distant past as Israel's conceptual motor.

Route 2 connects Tel Aviv and Haifa and runs along the sea. Heading north, after having left behind Tel Aviv's suburbs, one can see to the right some of the oldest kibbutzim in the country, whose lands still produce the fruits, vegetables, and flowers that Israel exports in great quantities around the world. As one comes closer to the Carmel hills, the fields are replaced by some of the most reputable vineyards in the country, planted by the Rothschild family at the end of the nineteenth century. To the left of the road one can see in rapid succession the Roman ruins of Caesarea with its amphitheater, the ruins of an Ottoman fortress, and farther up a small cape with an imposing fortress, also dating from the Ottoman era, now transformed into Israel's ultrasecret navy base. The Matam high-tech center rises a bit farther north on the same route, not unlike a mirage on the horizon. The center incarnates continuity through rupture because it no longer pursues the agricultural and military activities serviced by Route 2.

Israel's civil research has of course profited immensely from the spillovers of its military research with its constant innovation in the fields of communications and security. The young Israeli entrepreneurs who dominate the start-up field practically all possess the same elite double curriculum: study at the prestigious Technion of Haifa, followed by military service in the army's ultrasecret scientific units. They have never experienced war from inside a tank, or, for the older entrepreneurs, in the units that were posted next to Sabra and Chatila, much less those in charge of patrolling the checkpoints surrounding the Palestinian Authority. The start-ups have also benefited greatly from the country's agronomic research, driven by the need to solve the chronic problem of water shortage and the minute size of the country's agricultural land.

It may come as a surprise, but in reality, the new high-tech start-ups are much closer in nature to the old trades that prevailed inside Jewish life in the Diaspora than to the technological and agricultural models that proudly symbolized the early years of Israel's state building when self-sufficiency was the order of the day in the 1950s and 1960s. Venture capitalists coming mainly from outside Israel, from the "inferior" Diaspora, provided the necessary investment capital for Israel's start-ups. The new companies that have mushroomed throughout Israel in the last decade all share the same characteristics: a creativity based on the openness and the interconnections of an Internet society that disregards all national borders; an unbeatable value-added content that is often delocalized, based on high mobility and with very few material ties to the physical spot where its activities are taking place; a flexible space/time schedule that eschews any heavy infrastructure and any heavy bureaucratic base.

Israel's old agronomy, the one of the much heralded orange and avocado miracles, sang the praises of an ever deeper rooting in the nation's soil, whereas the military values of the young state were all based on the notion of defendable terrestrial borders. The new technology instead is all about mobility and flexibility, with little, if any, anchoring in any soil or with any clear national identity. Can this change hearken back to the Middle Ages when the Jews, before their emancipation, incarnated these same values in the financial and commercial realm? The new start-ups have as clients, technological global giants rather than individual consumers around the world, who still remain anchored in their respective national settings. Does this strategic choice echo in its own way the old Jewish tradition of dialoguing with kings rather than with their people?[7] Google could certainly qualify as a new type of king . . . and might the fear of individual consumer boycotts replicate the age-old Jewish fear of an uncontrollable vox populi? These start-ups, by the way, have no desire to become big companies tied down by heavy staffs and a bureaucratic context in any given national setting, not even an Israeli one. Those who create them sell them off once the products they offer are integrated inside new global technologies. One can even wonder, within the scale of Western time, whether the technological know-how these start-ups contain in their microchips isn't today's equivalent of those polished diamonds that Jews in the past could carry from one country to another in their travels or expulsions.

Looking to the future, one can imagine that given Israel's military high tech, Israelis could reach a moment in time when peace with their neighbors could be possible because the state's terrestrial borders, so hotly disputed since its creation, might lose all of their protective symbolism. Many already think this is the case, but the vast majority of Israelis still want, and understandably so, secure and visible borders, given the fact that any new technological alternatives would be, by definition, top secret. But in this context, the struggle of one part of the Israeli population to hang on to the occupied lands of "Judea and Samaria" no longer has much to do with security needs, and is based only on the desire to restore and hang on to an ancient terrestrial biblical identity.

There is no better proof of this intertwining of technological future and biblical past than the large numbers of young, highly orthodox entrepreneurs who are perfectly capable of conjugating their economic and technological start-ups with the most strictly observant Jewish family life, where children have no access to television or the Internet. These young entrepreneurs can remain totally faithful to their biblical understanding of time and space because the Internet has abolished the old Industrial Revolution's rigid categories of work hours and workplace, proposing instead a new cybernetic fusion of the two. The lightness of their work instruments allows them to devote themselves to the heaviness of their religious precepts. The same holds true for the growing number of Haredi women (but no men, for the time being) who are encouraged to take on technical jobs in the computer realm. A fascinating example of how Talmudic scholars keep up with technological progress: the current intellectual and religious reflections taking place at Bar-

Ilan University on whether Tefillin (the leather straps that connect the forehead with the right arm, which orthodox men put on to pray) should be wrapped around a cybernetic artificial arm, or what to do if improperly harnessed brain waves accidentally turn on a light on the Shabbat.[8] This is how Israel can reconcile the Talmud with its old Zionist heritage in order to keep the allegiance of all of its citizens. In so doing, the old cleavages between religious and secular camps lose all meaning. Ben-Gurion and Rav Cook must cohabit on the Internet if Israel wishes to hang on to its national copyright.

But what will Israel's future be among nations and in particular in its own geographical neighborhood? The country's nanotechnological sector has produced the first "nano-Bible": The Torah and the Koran fit onto a chip no larger than a speck of dust. This nano-Bible was offered to Pope Benedict XVI as a small token of interreligious friendship—even though it did not contain the New Testament.[9] The contrast with those Koranic schools in Pakistan or Afghanistan where children are taught to recite the Koran in Arabic by heart, even though they do not understand a word of it, is striking.

It is true that there are some start-ups in the realm of banking and health that have been set up in Haifa where young Israeli Arabs with the proper technical degrees can find jobs. But these young Arabs, who do not generally serve in the army (which is the key national melting pot) and would not be accepted in its elite corps, cannot work in the vast majority of the country's high-tech start-ups.[10] Therefore the few start-ups willing to hire them, rather than calming their frustration, may actually increase in the long run these young Arabs' feeling of alienation toward Israeli democracy in what Tocqueville called the revolution of expectations. I don't know whether the Palestinians on the other side will ever benefit from all of this advanced technology in their own suggested national "start-up." But one thing is clear: the Israeli government is going forward with the construction of ever larger settlements in what were Palestinian lands and plans to construct 2,500 new apartments in East Jerusalem alone.[11] Will Israel, which uses cement to carry out national policy, rely on its high technology to finish off the job? For the only Palestinian state that can exist in the future will clearly be a "nano-state."

The Matam center physically turns its back to the Israeli hinterland and to the Israeli-Palestinian conflict. Planted practically at the edge of the sea, its gaze is resolutely turned toward the setting sun in the West, but a sun that sets well beyond Europe, the high-tech pygmy. One is tempted to say that Matam, in its twinning with its Californian brothers, who sit on the other side of the San Andreas fault, also turning their backs to the rest of the United States, is also turning its sights toward that extreme West, which morphs seamlessly into the Far East of the future: a future already lived as a daily reality in an Israel that thinks of itself as an aquarium, as a bubble, and as a tent.

6

THE AQUARIUM

The summer evening has that special freshness so unique to Jerusalem: perfect temperature, a light wind wafting the cool air as newly planted olive and cypress trees sway gently in chorus in front of the ramparts of the Old City. I am sitting at a table in a restaurant at the heart of the new Mamilla shopping mall: a vast pedestrian street that begins a few steps away from Jaffa Gate and ends by the French Saint Vincent Hospice at the beginning of Jaffa Road, the road that led to Jaffa by the sea, well before Tel Aviv had even been conceived.

A crowd is strolling peacefully in the mall as though without a care in the world. Entire families (even with young children in strollers), young couples, groups of adolescents, and mature couples are all out in the mild night, window-shopping in front of stores that display the latest clothing fashions, summer shoes, and trendy household objects, before stopping for an ice cream or an American cookie. The scene could be taking place anywhere in the up-and-coming areas of the world, but paradoxically not in the United States, where the very first shopping malls have aged, and not so gracefully. I think instead of Bangalore's newest shopping mall, inaugurated more or less at the same time as Mamilla: the same appetite for novelty, the same youthful crowds, the same boutiques carrying global trademarks surrounded in the less fancy sites by smaller ones carrying local labels, including a state-of-the-art huge pharmacy that sells generic *made in Israel* drugs, not unlike those *made in India,* at very competitive prices. Israel, of course, is not India. But as the summer tent movement showed, the income gap between rich and poor in Israel has reached previously unimaginable levels, destroying in the process the relative egalitarianism that used to prevail in the country. And as in India, the commercial center in Jerusalem is very close to another reality: the Arab Quarter of East Jerusalem with its eternal bazaars, its shop sellers sitting on plastic chairs in front of piles of clothing, rugs, silver jewels, ceramic objects, dried fruits, spices, and mountains of watermelons.

There are young Arabs from East Jerusalem among the strollers in this open-air shopping mall. A group of young women wearing blue jeans and the hijab, thanks to which they can be distinguished from their Israeli Jewish peers, walk by, and one can spot a few families, but there are no elderly. It is just the opposite among the Jewish ultraorthodox. They too are strolling, but one sees only very young couples with their children or mature, even elderly, adults, but no young singles. These are still under parental control and no one wants them to compromise the group's strict principles. Were they to be spotted in a shopping mall, their ultraorthodoxy would be questioned and their marriage prospects would wilt. One can see these young singles strolling in the streets of West Jerusalem, their mothers walking in front, the young man with his large black hat and the young girl with a dark-hued ankle-length dress a few steps behind. These outings, I am told, are timed. The times such a young couple can be out together can be counted on the fingers of one hand before they must decide whether they are made for each other. Their body language during these determining encounters is fascinating: they walk with a clearly visible distance between them, and both keep their arms crossed over their chests. In our Western world such a gesture denotes mistrust and unwillingness to cooperate. In their universe, it must instead convey purity and seriousness.

The young Palestinians who have come down the ramparts into the shopping mall are technically speaking at home, if one takes at face value the pronouncements of Israel's political class with its assertion that Jerusalem will remain "united forever." But the presence of these young Arabs does not go entirely unnoticed, because it jars with habits developed since the Second Intifada when any Arab in the street bred panic for fear that he or she might be a suicide bomber.[1] But on this balmy June evening their presence in the shopping center seems to confirm what some of my Israeli friends are constantly telling me: the "situation" is not as bad as proclaimed by those who seek to delegitimize Israel. There can be peaceful interactions in daily life. I notice that there has been no (visible) check before entering the garage underneath the shopping mall and no controls as one entered the mall itself. But then again, who knows what brand new invisible technological innovation is doing the job. The security guard in front of the restaurant gives the impression of being far more interested in ensuring that clients get a table outside than in checking their handbags, which he contemplates with the same casual indifference of his Western peers. But here, I tell myself, we are at the very heart of the problem . . . not at its margins. Or am I once again stuck in my antiquated geography? Should I believe what many Israelis tell me, that things are quite different when looked at up close?

I remember that during my East Talpiot lesson three weeks earlier, my ultraorthodox friend had mentioned the Mamilla shopping center as problematic. I now understand his reasons and doubly so. If the youths of East Jerusalem start coming here regularly, they will not head out to Ramallah to strengthen their start-up nation as my friend hopes. And if the ultraorthodox also start coming to this mall where scantily clad young women stroll by, what will happen to their strict principles and above all to their slightly antiquated Spartan stores in their neighborhood of Mea Shearim? Israel would no longer be engaged in a massive game of Go but would find itself caught up instead in a zero-sum game devoid of all teleological meaning—but one that, to my eyes at least, would be full of historical (and secular) hope.

The Mamilla neighborhood today has nothing in common with the old Arab and Jewish Quarter before 1949 where Theodore Herzl stayed during his trip to Palestine. It also bears no resemblance to the no-man's-land it became after the armistice of 1949, when on the Israeli side one always ran the danger of being hit by Jordanian fire. As a result, this highly central neighborhood sank into virtual disarray and became a place where the poorest Jewish immigrants from North Africa settled and opened small garages and repair shops. It took more than forty years after the 1967 war for this neighborhood to be transformed into one of the most elegant areas of a newly trendy Jerusalem with its lot of luxury hotels. The apartment buildings that now dot Mamilla, with their breathtaking views of the Old City ramparts and David's Tower, were sold for astronomical prices to the richest Jews of the Diaspora, who generally only spend a few weeks a year there. Trendy world culture has taken over what used to be the wasteland between Mamilla and the Mishkenot Sha'ananim: a new open-air amphitheater hosts music and opera concerts—Dame Kiri te Kanawa had just sung there a few days before. The architects behind all of these complexes had the good taste to hide the shopping mall behind a terraced wall whose landscaped greenery offers a gentle contrast to the violent (when one knows the history) starkness of the Old City ramparts. As a result, one can window-shop in front of the Tommy Hilfiger or the Rolex boutique a few steps away from the Ottoman ramparts and right next to the Christian

bastions our canon of a century ago praised as the peaceful in-
carnations of a new gentle crusading spirit.

I do not know how to react to this shopping mall. Its atmosphere is at once extraordinary and so very normally casual. I
am torn between joy and malaise. Joy because Mamilla marks
the triumph of calm well-being where for two decades the ste-
rility of a no-man's-land and, more recently, the fear of terrorist
attacks had ruled—but malaise in front of so much luxury and
voluptuousness in a region best described as a powder keg, surrounded by explosives. I cannot shed the feeling that Israel is
living somehow at the antipodes of its birthplace, as if the walls
of the city were no more than very beautiful theatrical decors.
In my nightmares the shopping mall could well turn out to be
nothing more than a cement mirage and this stroll amidst such
consumer pleasure the result of a frightening insouciance in front
of a tragedy that is still lurking behind the curtains.

I turn to my dinner companion, a well-known Israeli social
scientist with a European social democratic background. His
research in Israeli and Palestinian demography played a role in
Ariel Sharon's decision to leave Gaza, for if one wanted Israel to
remain both "Jewish and democratic," the state had to contain
far fewer Arabs. "Jewish and democratic" implies an impossible
political and philosophical squaring of the circle. Nevertheless,
it has become a mantra that conveys perfectly the aspirations of
the vast majority of Jewish Israelis. The concept has therefore
taken on a reality of its own in this peculiar land and it will be
difficult to dismantle it.

My interlocutor has become an expert on the territorial exchanges that would have to be made if the two-state solution is
to be implemented. He has pleaded on its behalf for many years.
He is convinced that it is urgent to carry it out now but considers it ever less likely because the political leadership does not
really want it. So, he too now spends time reflecting on the

future of the Jewish people beyond Israel. In his Zionist youth, he considered any Jew who did not immigrate to Israel the equivalent of a dead leaf destined to fall off the Jewish tree at the slightest wind. Now instead, he has taken to thinking of the Jewish world as a series of ever wider concentric circles of belonging, the last of which could very well be the *conversos* of Portuguese and Spanish origin whose ancestors were forced to abandon their Jewish faith from the late fifteenth to the early eighteenth century, and whose descendants are increasingly interested in finding and retracing their Jewish roots. He smiles when he tells me that there are probably 80 million of them around, a nice bulwark that could protect the officially declared Jews whose 13 million constitute, he insists, less than the statistical error of the Chinese census.

The times have truly changed. In the past, those who abandoned their Judaism, for whatever reason, had only one goal, to run away from it by embracing the host culture, including the religious and cultural antisemitism of its elites. Now they are more than eager to learn more about their past identities. Nor is it a coincidence that my recently retired interlocutor has taken on the responsibility of preparing the dossiers of potential candidates for the status of "the Righteous" of Yad Vashem, Israel's memorial and study center for the victims of the Holocaust. And it is with the smile of a European connoisseur that he tells me that the entire procedure of furnishing proof and counter-proof of a non-Jew saving at the risk of his own life a Jew during the Holocaust strangely resembles the Vatican's procedure for beatification, the first step toward canonization. In Judaism however, the miracle is human and therefore far more rare.

Sitting in the middle of the shopping mall, I wonder whether, in this Israel that has increasingly moved into a world of economic well-being and individually oriented consumer lifestyles, the reference to the Holocaust may not be gradually losing significance. If that were the case, then we would be living the very last avatars of a generational moment. To return to the Möbius strip metaphor, the Holocaust may be in the process of sinking behind the strip's underside, replaced by a renewed Talmudic reading of the past, one that also eschews the essentially secular reading of the Bible as national literature of the early years of the state.

In the restaurant, I contemplate a young woman wearing a hijab who has just walked in to order a latte macchiato at the bar. Next to her an ultraorthodox couple in their fifties is reading the menu with that stern and serious look that their indirect descendants, the Puritans and the Calvinists of yore, displayed when painted by the Dutch masters. Next to them, a cluster of youths in T-shirts are laughing merrily at a long convivial table. The young and lovely waitress, who speaks perfect English, comes to our table and suggests the day's menu, replete with its Italian and Thai names, to which she adds a French onion soup and the ever-present Caesar salad (why not call it *Herod's Salad* here?). We are in the midst of *world food,* so much so that there is no hummus or trina on the menu, too provincial in the restaurateur's trendy eyes.

The restaurant scene seems idyllic. This juxtaposition of Arabs, lay, and ultraorthodox Jews makes me think of London or Canada, two worlds that define themselves as multicultural (perhaps, in the English case, in the past). And what if peace were to come about in dozens of shopping malls around a macchiato? I ask the question to my interlocutor. He smiles wanly to display his skepticism. He tells me the country is doing too well for the Israelis to feel the need for peace. It could only disturb a highly pleasant status quo. And then he warns against false comparisons. The presence in the same public space of so many different protagonists must not be equated with what goes on in a European or North American city, where the same individuals would be spurred to meaningful political interaction because society and the state would not allow them as citizens to live out their entire lives inside their own group in their respective corners. "Here instead, we are in an aquarium," he tells me.

All of a sudden I contemplate Jerusalem in an entirely different manner. I see it as one of those very large and ultrasophisticated aquariums with, at the bottom, many little decorative and kitschy objects such as old stones and a few amphorae, all highlighted by refined lighting, not unlike the lighting that is illuminating the walls of the Old City in front of our terrace. In these waters, amply oxygenated by the outside world (one thinks of the millions of dollars and euros that are injected in this aquarium), all types and sizes of highly colored fish, each going toward a specific destination, swim about while turning rapidly away to avoid the others, and all of this in utter silence. My interlocutor smiles when he sees my surprise, and then adds as a final touch: "It is not a very convivial metaphor, but it can work . . . provided there are no baby piranhas in their midst."

The silence of the aquarium was something I had already experienced a year earlier in a conference at the University of Haifa Law School. This city and its university are considered to be Israel's most multicultural spot because of their strong Israeli Arab and Druze presence. And indeed, on the campus one could see quite a few Arab students—mainly young women—virtually all wearing the hijab to underscore their identity—walking peacefully about on their way to class or to the cafeteria, but always as a group and with no Israeli Jews in their midst. When I tried to learn more about these Arab students—their backgrounds and where they were heading in professional terms—by asking some of their professors and above all their assistants (I had no direct access to the students, because I was participating in an international conference), I was surprised by the vagueness of their replies. They knew very little, if anything, about these students they saw every day. And these students, who except for some Druzes had no access to Israel's military service, would inevitably find themselves on the margins of Israeli society, destined to become mainly professionals for their own Arab ilk: to each fish its own itinerary.

Yet all of my interlocutors were convinced they were participating in a highly successful multicultural experiment. They did not realize that they were adding an extra layer of controversy to a term that is rapidly losing its luster in our Western democratic societies. I still remember the two friendly dinners with the conference participants. The first one took place by the Haifa port in a trendy restaurant owned by a Christian Arab homosexual who had made it a point to turn it into an oasis of tolerance. He welcomed us warmly but with an elliptical speech during which he presented the restaurant's history as a resident of Haifa without mentioning the word "Israel" even once.

The smile on the faces of the Druzes who welcomed us in their restaurant high up on the hills behind Haifa were just as tourist inclined, only even more enigmatic. They seemed to be wearing the same masks as the restaurateurs of Abu Gosh in the past with the Saturday tourists from Jerusalem. They made me think of the coldness with which Druze dignitaries who had been invited to the very first Presidential Conference in Jerusalem in 2008, the year of Israel's sixtieth anniversary, reacted to President George Bush's "200 Percent Behind Israel" speech. A caricaturist on the spot would have drawn them as so many stalagmites patiently waiting to meet up with their Lebanese Druze brothers/stalactites in a time frame that bore no relation to our Western journalistic or even historical time.

I try to come back to my senses. Here in the aquarium I am surely going nowhere with my European and American references. I should start all over again. Maybe one should be thinking of Israel as a posthumous splinter of the old Ottoman

Empire, one that allows its ethnic non-Jewish populations to live somewhat honorable and free lives, even if they remain parallel to mainstream society. The rule of law in such a context does not include the basic building block of democratic pluralism: full equality of all citizens. The famous elderly Israeli political scientist Shlomo Avineri always stressed that Israel was "of" Europe but not "in" Europe. As a member of the old Zionist social-democratic camp, he defined Israel's distancing in geocultural, not political, terms, given the fact that Israel lived in a geographical context where many of its neighbors sought its destruction, but as far as democratic principles went, Avineri remained squarely in the Western camp. But since 2000, according to some left-wing researchers, the Israeli-Palestinian conflict has been transformed. It is no longer centered on territorial issues linked to borders but increasingly on what can be called ethnic borders. This change has affected the very nature of Israel's pluralist democracy and its rule of law.[2]

Nowadays perhaps a new coherence is in order. If Israel moves toward Asia, then, there is no point measuring its political performance with our Western values. Besides, its full-fledged proportionally representative system, a last poisoned gift of Poland's interwar heritage, bears no relation to Europe's system of politically corrected majorities designed to avoid all extremes. Nor do we have in Europe parties with ultrareligious agendas. So it is necessary to change orientation. The aquarium can be a dream model for many of the globe's emerging nations. It would be an unexpected paradise for all those ethnic or religious dissidents in authoritarian countries, such as Russia and China, or in search of a bit more freedom, as in Thailand or Burma. Populations there would all love to be swimming in aquariums without piranhas and where the bigger fish would contemplate them with indifference. Israel, in its move, could thus become the teacher of such an Asian classroom—provided it remains faithful to the rule of law principles and fulfills the expectations of its tent movement, while also taking into account the far more complex needs of its Arab citizens. Might the Indian model of pacifist struggle prove useful to the latter?

There is a definite Gandhian perfume in the air among many Palestinians who are fighting to keep their lands, according to an Israeli activist.[3] He spends a lot of time in the Palestinian olive groves in the Hebron area defending the workers who try to take care of their trees or seek access to their wells. His purpose: to prevent by his presence the armed settlers from shooting at the Palestinians. These armed Israelis refuse to call themselves "settlers" because they consider themselves as Israel's pioneer front line in the battle to reconquer legitimate lands that, according to the Bible, belong to Israel. And it is no accident that this activist is one of the world's leading specialists on India.

With the activists by their sides, the Palestinian workers are no longer easy targets for settler fire, for the latter do not want to get negative publicity for their movement by shooting at an Israeli. It is the army that has the dirty job of retaliating against these Israeli citizens who dare to combat the settlers. These peaceful protesters are routinely charged for having "trespassed in a military security zone." And the perimeter of this so-called zone is quite flexible depending on the situation, whereas the settlers are nearly never disturbed or arrested. I realize that my interlocutor speaks of the Israeli army the way an Indian would have spoken before independence of the British army. But with a major difference: it is *his* army, the one in which he also served when he was younger. I ask him whether his movement is succeeding. He looks at me calmly before telling me that he does what he can to help the laborers who are the victims of history. He does not harbor many illusions, but at least he is at peace with his conscience. And he finds some hope in the new nonviolent methods that are gaining favor within the Palestinian Authority.[4]

One can ask whether these new nonviolent methods will not slowly change the Israeli landscape both internally with the tent movement and externally with the Palestinian marches. But these manifestations do not seem to have stopped the authoritarian currents in the government, which have found their spokesman in Avigdor Lieberman, the current minister of foreign affairs and the chairman of the nationalist party, Yisrael Beitenou, whose members, many from the former Soviet Union, seem to adhere to the classical conservative American line: "My country, love it or leave it." They have even submitted a bill in the Israeli Parliament to require a loyalty oath from all of Israel's citizens, above all the Arab population.[5] As a result, other Palestinian voices are beginning to rise against what they perceive as a pernicious climate of soft "normalization" without any real burning issue ever being addressed, much less solved, in the Israeli-Palestinian conflict.[6]

As I sit in the restaurant with a breathtaking view of one of the most beautiful places on earth, I cannot help but wonder just how watertight this Israeli aquarium is. And I understand why the vast majority of Israel's non-ultraorthodox youths live on a day-by-day basis and dream of taking long exotic trips once their army service is over. They are fish, who would like to swim, if only once, in natural waters. I also understand the title of Etgar Keret and Shira Geffe's film, *The Jellyfish,* which won the Golden Camera Award in Cannes in 2007. The film depicts the drab lives of three Tel Aviv women, one of whom is Filipino, as they go about their jobs and their family lives. These women one day meet a mysterious little girl who has just come out of the sea and who will return just as mysteriously and as silently into the sea at the end of the film. Aquariums do not have jellyfish—those gelatinous invertebrates that sting, and can even kill, belong to the sea's deep currents. Out there in the great open spaces lurk natural dangers that Israel, accustomed above all to human dangers, has never had to confront.

Can one live daily in a world where one has to constantly square circles? Geometry is a severe and thankless discipline that can be studied only in small quantities. When it becomes an existential discipline, its curves and angles can prove suffocating. True, some problems have no solutions. Many Israelis ask with only a slightly provocative tone why one has to find at all costs a solution to the Israel-Palestinian conflict, and they point to Cyprus, which remains divided to this day and with no solution in sight. True. But in places that are also palimpsests, the struggle between competing memories becomes ever fiercer with time and turns into an emotional knot whose political repercussions can explode at any moment.

The Old City of Jerusalem *intra muros* is such a place. The piranhas have already come and gone, but they can always return, and I do not know whether the young Palestinian woman with her hijab who came down to the shopping mall from the 'other side' to order her macchiato incarnates an exceptional moment or is the first harbinger of a calm future.

7

THE BUBBLE

The sushi restaurant is on an esplanade between two impressive ultramodern towers in the ancient freight depot area of Tel Aviv. Different types of Asian colored fish swim in the aquarium, the restaurant's most important decoration. The human aquarium is to be found sitting at the tables. Tel Aviv is no longer the young secular city whose first century was celebrated in 2009, the antithesis to eternally pious Jerusalem. Bnei Brak, the ultrareligious satellite city, home of the sages one still reads during the Passover ritual, is nearby, and besides the city already had a highly observant religious population, before the exiled German Jews gave it its modern character. Today its business towers and its world economy increasingly attract the ultrareligious from the entire world. One can spot several of them eating their raw fish in the restaurant, either among men or as couples sitting a bit sullenly in quasi-religious silence.

The restaurant is quite far away from the Tel Aviv University campus, but it is the only one that will do for our small group of academics. The respondent to my lecture is none other than my ultraorthodox friend who gave me the "lesson from East Talpiot," and the Tel Aviv organizers had to find a restaurant where he, who keeps *Glatt Kosher*, could eat, the simple "kosher" qualification of most Israeli restaurants not being sufficient for him. That is how three members of the social science faculty of Tel Aviv University, all three ultrasecular in outlook, managed (just about) the squaring of the circle. The chosen restaurant had to comply with two major constraints: financial for the research center and religious for the respondent, and of course both converged. *Glatt Kosher* restaurants are far more expensive because the products they use require a more careful selection and extra handling. The academics finally found a reasonably priced restaurant that followed *Glatt* precepts but did not possess the appropriate rabbinical imprimatur. Our friend, after a telephone conversation with the chef, agreed to go there. I asked him what had convinced him that he could eat in such a restaurant. His reply was to the point: the chef made sure that there was not the slightest little organism in the salads and the vegetables. It seems that in principle, *Glatt Kosher* implies that the lungs of all animals that are butchered according to religious ritual must be free of even the slightest lesion or defect. But as with many other injunctions in highly orthodox Judaism, in order to ensure that the injunction is perfectly respected, the interdictions are extended to a far larger set of rules.[1] *Glatt* purity now covers all food. I smile as I listen to my friend's explanation: ensuring that salads do not contain the smallest living insect gives me an added argument for my feeling that Israel is moving closer to Confucian Asia: hadn't the Buddha forbidden pilgrimages during the insect reproducing season, for fear that the pilgrims might crush them during their long walks?

We sit at the table. The Tel Aviv academics barely knew the term *Glatt* before the evening, and they are all contemplating my friend with ethnological curiosity. The evening's conversation inevitably focuses on the misunderstandings between lay and religious Israelis. My ultrareligious friend is convinced that the secular camp looks upon his "black" peers with contempt. The academics fight back: on the contrary, it is the "blacks" who shun them. I listen to the conversation as a double ethnologist. No one is uttering the word "tensions," and everybody around the table makes a special effort to underscore that they all belong to the same Jewish people. There is a minuet-like style to the conversation: highly civilized exchanges that imply two steps forward toward the other, followed by one step back. The unity of time is dictated by the vicissitudes of Israeli life and the formalism comes from the gestures at the table. As my friend does not shake women's hands, the secular hosts had, something quite rare for Israel, actually prepared a seating arrangement that allowed him to sit between two men.

With the help of the Japanese food, beer, and sake, conviviality finally won the day. The secular academics laughed heartily when my friend explained to them, with a bit of provocation, that they all shared the same Israeli highway but in different cars and with different speeds, the ultraorthodox (of course in his eyes) in a Rolls Royce, the others in compact cars, and even in Trabants. Everyone agreed that they shared the same ultimate goal and accepted the following sentence: "What counts is that we are all heading in the same direction and want the same thing: the well-being of the Jewish people and Israel's survival, the enemies being at our door." The dinner ended by evoking a hypothetical event (which would have been beyond the realm of the imagination in the past, but which might occur one day): a pacific march of one million Gaza citizens on Tel Aviv, the worst possible scenario in the game of Go—the Chinese strategic game based on the encircling of the enemy that my ultraorthodox friend had evoked during my "lesson from East Talpiot."

Perhaps one should also welcome them peacefully, argued not without some irony, a researcher with a poetic countenance who clearly came from the old Argentinian extreme left. "Who knows," he added, "maybe after a small tour of the city, they will go back quietly to their homes." The other guests around the table looked at him with fear in their eyes, as if he had suddenly proclaimed his intention to embrace tigers. A dinner participant with Sephardic origins ended the conversation by pointing as we walked out to the towers outside while posing a rhetorical question: "How many other miracles could Israel have produced, if only it had not been surrounded by Arabs?"

"If only. . . ." She made it sound as though it were only a technical detail. Tel Aviv has always lived as though protected by a bubble. And indeed its inhabitants have often called the city "The Bubble" because it seemed to live outside Israeli reality. This is the title of Eytan Fox's 2006 film, which describes the lives and love affairs of gay young Israeli men, one of them with a Palestinian, and their female friends in a trendy city seeking peace with the Second Intifada and suicide bombers not just as background but as the end of the story. Unlike Jerusalem, Tel Aviv has never had to contend with an important Arab presence, those in Jaffa being a relatively small minority with little, if any, political weight. Jaffa has been transformed. Real estate agents now call it "the Jaffa scene" because the promontory has become one of Tel Aviv's most elegant residential neighborhoods, with terraced penthouses whose prices have skyrocketed. I quote arbitrarily from one real estate ad:

> You've Seen Nothing Yet. *Top of Jaffa:* In the heart of the Jaffa scene. Immediate occupancy. 12 penthouses and roof top apartments with an enormous balcony, on one level. Amazing choice, of size (up to 564 square meters) and of price (NIS 3.4 million). Situated between Pisgah Garden and the famous flea market, high up above the sea, under the brilliant blue sky, which becomes ignited with pink and golden fire at sunset, followed by an evening of dazzling stars.[2]

Tel Aviv as a city without obstacles, capable of growing in all directions and with the sea as oxygen, contrary to conflicting, complex, and confined Jerusalem. Tel Aviv whose port was transferred to Ashdod and whose old railway station served no purpose, was able to convert the two into California fun spots:

a Santa Monica boardwalk along the sea and a trendy and picturesque neighborhood around the old railroad station, with
only the bus depot remaining as a vital connection with the rest
of the real country "out there."

In the shadow of the new skyscrapers and of the new Israel
on the move, the old Tel Aviv of the immigrants who arrived
from the four corners of Europe is unraveling before one's eyes.
The towers are shooting up at incredible speed, along with the
prices per square meter, which have reached vertiginous heights.
Entire neighborhoods are transformed as cranes work around
the clock, while the past vanishes. The Bauhaus "white city"
inscribed in the UNESCO patrimony of humanity is still there,
but the descendants of the German Jewish families, the *Jekkes*,
who built it, have either disappeared into the larger Israeli melting pot or they have come closer to Germany, whose citizenship
they have often reclaimed. Few notice the plaque in front of a
café on Rothschild Boulevard whose lines incarnate the existential strength and courage of a besieged German Jewry: *"Proudly
founded in 1934."* Europe's tragedies gave birth to the city's
cultural life: the theater and dance of the Russian avant-gardes;
German music (minus Wagner, for a long time) and architecture;
Viennese coffeehouses, Polish restaurants; and multilingual
bookstores, whose only avatars today carry Russian-language
products, but mainly videos rather than books. The progressive
European world that gave the city the lovely name "Spring
Hill" has disappeared. Its remnants now belong to a museum-
like past: one can take walking tours of the city that rose out of
the dunes, the Bauhaus buildings, the first houses where the
leaders, the bureaucrats, and the trade unions of the Jewish pre-
state kernel (the *Yishuv*) in British-mandated Palestine worked
and where they proclaimed Israel's independence in 1948.
Meanwhile the precious books, works of art, pianos, furniture,
and objects dating back to that period, which the first Russian

and German immigrants managed to bring with them, have now left the antique stores of Tel Aviv to resume their diasporic journey to the houses, offices, and museums of world-class collectors. The art market has witnessed more back-and-forth movement than history . . . for the time being.

Today's Tel Aviv has moved beyond all of these Old World anchors. Emboldened by the country's strength and by the coming-of-age of a new "bling-bling" generation of Israelis and world Jews who can actually pay the current real estate prices, the city now defines itself in vertical terms, and above all by the vast lobbies of its towers with their gaudy crystal chandeliers, their golden doorknobs—worthy of Moscow, Dubai, or Shanghai. The city has now rediscovered and restored the old neighborhoods to the south whose villas reflected a quaint pastiche of neo-Ottoman, Asian, and Central European architectural trends, at the antipodes of the German Bauhaus. Neve Tsedek, the shabby neighborhood surrounding the old train station, has become the place to go, with its small houses now turned into fashionable boutiques that, as everywhere else in the elegant consumer-driven world, now display exotic olive oils, perfumes, massaging lotions, some collectors' items, and the usual collection of minimalist dresses on minimalist hangers in purposefully empty spaces. Here and there one can spot French-like cafés and tea shops decorated to convey a mythical world of grandmothers and their homemade jams and cakes, as if the past between 1933 and 1945 no longer belonged to the Jewish existential tragedy but now came with a nostalgic aura. The city above all has become one of the trendiest cities in the world for its night life and partying spirit, ranking third in the 2011 list of "Top Ten Cities" in the *Lonely Planet* guide.[3] Even Easyjet, the trendy European low-cost airline, now flies there.

Time moves on, and at the lower end of the city at the crossroads between Allenby Street and Rothschild Boulevard one

can still spot small two-story houses with closed shutters await-
ing demolition. They are the last silent and moving witnesses of
so much hope and so much suffering and above all so much individual and family determination. Next to them one can still
see equally old small prayer halls whose paint has flaked, whose
windows are cracked and whose doors are kept shut with heavy
locks, replete with chalk graffiti. These buildings give the impression of having being transported from a *Shtetl* in the Ukraine.
But here the ravages of time denote no ancestral hatred of the
Jews, no historical oblivion, no collective pogroms and murders. The children of the original congregants simply moved on
and built their lives elsewhere in the city or the country: echoes
of Manhattan in the 1960s when new generations of Jews left
the Lower East Side and the turn-of-the-century immigrant
Jewish memories of Orchard Street for better lives in the subur-
ban American dream.

Will the social science building at Tel Aviv University suffer
the same fate? The professor with East European origins, who
is still a fervent social democrat and such a Germanophile that
he spends his vacations in Berlin, seems to think so. He has just
written a book on Tel Aviv's history, and he has explained to me
the origins of many of its districts, including the green and
peaceful one near the university, built, he tells me, as there are
no traces left, on the site of an ancient Arab village. I detect a
certain historical sadness in his gaze, as though Israel could
have been born, or could have at least grown, differently. But it
is he who on our way to the sushi restaurant pointed to the hills
on the horizon as if to better stress the folly of the idea: "And
over there, one day, it should become Palestinian land." I measure the complexity of his inevitably schizophrenic gaze full of
generous sentiments on behalf of the Arab past but also of sheer
fear over the future.

History has left its toll on his outlook just as it has in the social science faculty and in the university. My interlocutor contemplates with sadness the building where his institute is located: it reeks of the fatigued modernity of the 1960s with its narrow dysfunctional and nondescript corridors, its minute offices that resemble so many cages, its small windows, the flaky paint, the outdated Spartan metal furniture. And he compares it all with the modernity and luminosity of the new buildings that house the technological and computer institutes and the law and business school faculties: they all have large bay windows, vast amphitheaters, informal rest areas where students can congregate and work together, and welcoming cafeterias. I understand that, in his eyes, what is at stake is not the architecture but a certain existential raison d'être. He tells me that the very best students are no longer interested in the social sciences. They all want to go into business. This is pretty much true everywhere, but in Israel such individual choices entail far greater consequences. The very idea that one can improve society through greater forms of social justice and rational planning—which, pushed to their logical extremes, could one day also encompass Israel's own Arabs and the country's neighbors—has become outdated, even irrelevant. Hope has shifted to science and business, and globalization has done the rest.

The university, once the bastion of these secular Zionist hopes, has adapted to these new horizons even in its key symbolic buildings. The combined Cymbalista Synagogue and Jewish Heritage Center, the work of the Swiss architect Mario Botta, brings together under the same roof but in two separate areas, not unlike the two sides of an open Torah scroll, Ben-Gurion's grandchildren with those of Rav Kook. An open and peaceful dialogue has ensued. Even ultraorthodox Jews now feel at home on a campus that by espousing technical and business/law values allows them to pursue their own often inwardly closed religious life.

Beth Hatefutsot, formerly the Museum of the Jewish Diaspora, sits at the very heart of the campus. It was originally founded as the historical depository of the Zionist ideal. Israel's children could learn there about their very different geographic and historical origins while discovering the extent of their forefathers' diasporic suffering, so as to better appreciate their Israeli identity. The museum has been totally refurbished and has opened its doors in 2012 with a far less Zionist identity, as the Museum of the Jewish People. One no longer needs to settle in Israel to participate in the country's movement. A Russian billionaire who ended up settling in Israel now presides over the museum's board of directors. And it is another Russian billionaire who has given the money for the university's Institute of European Jewry, where I gave my lecture. This billionaire is currently the president of the European Jewish Congress, a title that speaks wonders concerning the representative nature of the institution, Russia not being exactly imbued with Europe's democratic values. But in Israel the term "Europe" refers above all to a geographic and an economic space. The postwar European project, with its values of reconciliation, freedom, and pluralist democracy, is at best a distant background noise that exerts little influence. Europe counts so little in Israel's planetary vision that confusing "Russia" with "Europe" does not even raise eyebrows.

The bubble that once used to protect only Tel Aviv, the beacon city of Israel's secular modernity, now covers (can it really protect?) the country as a whole. Last summer's tent movement did not really try to pierce it. Its activists sought merely to promote greater social justice among those who lived within its bounds. In order to maintain cohesion among the very different types of people inside the tent movement, no one dared to mention the Tartars next door. What would have been the point? The bubble's roof is open to the greater world. The air circulating inside it is planetary.

And as is always the case, when there is a conciliatory or peace-oriented mood, Arab terrorists (their origin is irrelevant) make it a point of honor to wreck it. The terrorist attacks near Eilat on August 18, 2011, turned most tent protesters once again into supporters of the conservative government for whom acts of terrorism are an unsolicited political manna falling from the sky. Thus in periods of peace as in those of tension, the bubble continues to protect the mentality of a population that seeks to live far from the region's madding crowd by avoiding any local interaction.

This is how Tel Aviv, the Bubble, has slowly taken over the entire country, thus turning it into a bubble-land, including Jerusalem, now happy and eager to define itself as much for its leisure activities as for its religious aura. The Mamilla shopping mall is just one example, but this desire to turn the city into a youthful and trendy place goes well beyond. The city now organizes its own film, dance, and opera festivals and even rock concerts.

The line was already quite long in front of the ticket office on Jaffa Road next to the city hall on a balmy Thursday afternoon, an hour before the concert. Behind large white screens that blocked access to the stage, one could hear the musicians preparing their instruments and testing their voices, their sounds amplified out into the street by large loudspeakers. Youths in "hip-hop" outfits, jeans, or hippy-like flowing robes were patiently licking ice cream, waiting to enter into the concert area.

Next to them a young ultraorthodox father was trying in vain to put his toddler son back into his stroller, to get him out of this scandalizing place as quickly as possible. The little boy would not hear of it. He stood there mesmerized by the music, the sounds, the young women's abundant hair, the strange clothing, and the relative nudity of the youths waiting in line. The young father was becoming ever more flustered and clearly did not know how to convince the little boy. Suddenly he grabbed his son like a parcel, strapped him in the stroller, and rushed away from temptation with what seemed to be giant steps. How many relevant Talmudic passages had gone through his mind before he reached this draconian decision? Not reading the secular press, with no television at home and not listening to the radio, how could he have known about the concert? He had clearly taken the wrong road back to his ultraorthodox neighborhood. As for the boy, clearly dazzled by the spectacle, will he one day step out of his ultraorthodox world? He could do so without leaving the city, for Jerusalem has stepped up its efforts to hang on to its secular Jews by offering them some night life.

The Yellow Submarine, situated in the midst of freight depots in a peripheral area of Jerusalem, is an ancestor. It was created twenty years ago and it has become the place in Jerusalem for rock, jazz, and soul concerts. Israel's best musical groups perform there, and it also serves as an incubator for new talent, musicians who go on to achieve fame in front of far larger audiences in Tel Aviv. But "the real creativity takes place here," says, with a bit of a haughty tone, the director of the club, a club whose dark atmosphere and musical vibrations could stand the comparison with its British or American equivalents. The public is knowledgeable, the songs part in Hebrew, part in English, are refined, and the music reflects the coming together of many cultures: Black, American, and Latino. One hears many different languages spoken, and the food is global: tapas have replaced hummus.

The evening is being held in honor of the Jerusalem Foundation, which helps to finance the club, and I am the guest of friends who are in town for the foundation's yearly meeting.

The Jerusalem Foundation is an international philanthropic organization whose purpose is to improve and enrich the lives of
all of Jerusalem's citizens, including the city's Arabs. The foundation's activities are praiseworthy: it finances the city's green
spaces, recreational centers for its poorer children, summer camps
for the handicapped, family planning and maternity centers, as
well as countless initiatives to get young Israelis and Palestinians to dialogue with each other. In brief, it is still very much a
child of the Oslo peace process spirit. Its sponsors are all wealthy
Jews from the Diaspora who still believe in the peace process
and who want Jerusalem to treat all of its citizens in an equal
manner. Some members of the group have a Teutonic profile:
they are non-Jewish German philanthropists who still belong to
the generation of responsibility. I wonder whether their children
will continue this commitment, and I notice that there are no
representatives of Germany's new (mainly former Soviet) Jewish
community. It comes as no surprise: they are mainly Jews who
refused to settle in Israel upon leaving the Soviet Union. Their
choice to move to Germany instead provoked considerable tension between Israel and the Federal Republic, until the Germans
made the Israelis understand that they simply could not refuse,
given the past, to take in Jews who sought to immigrate to their
country.

The Foundation, created one year before the 1967 victory,
supported all of Teddy Kollek's ideals and projects for a new
reunited Jerusalem. Forty-five years later, there is something
slightly anachronistic in these old European and North American Jewish philanthropic elites who congregate in the lobby of
the King David Hotel. They live outside the Israeli bubble and
are no longer in tune with the country's priorities today. Because they finance many useful projects, the national government and Jerusalem's City Hall let them continue their noble
pursuits. As a result, state money can be used to finance far

more political projects such as the expansion of the settlements around East Jerusalem. And these projects have found their ardent supporters among other types of Jews in the Diaspora. These other Jews are unconditional supporters of Benjamin "Bibi" Netanyahu and his international Likud movement, and they basically consider themselves as Israelis abroad. The old-style classical Jews of yore who defined themselves as stalwart and proud citizens of their respective countries while harboring both deep Zionist feelings and a belief in Western universal values are on the defensive now. The "new antisemitism" of the Arab street as shown in Europe during the Second Intifada, the Durban spirit, and the boycott of Israel movement have placed them in an awkward minority position vis -à-vis hard-line Jews who are happy to be fighting what they consider to be clear-cut and all-pervasive enemies.

One of the members of the Jerusalem Foundation confirms with a dose of sadness: "It is too bad the government destroys behind the scenes all that we try to do on behalf of the Palestinians in the city." She need say no more. The Yellow Submarine will survive, but I realize that in his presentation of its twenty years of the club's activity, the director never mentioned the presence of even one Israeli Arab or Palestinian group who might conjugate rock music with the Arab musical tradition, or one student who might have come to learn from the Beatles' spirit. It could very well be that young Arab voices may not wish to express themselves with such musical sounds or do not wish to cooperate with Israeli Jews. But I have the feeling that the "bubble" is simply not large enough to encompass them and that no one in this rock pantheon is willing to pursue the "Imagine" of John Lennon's song.

The bubble is closed but one can also leave it freely in order to pierce its confined sounds. This is the role of Israel's avant-garde artists. Many have chosen to leave the country and settle in Europe. The continent may have a negligible political presence in world affairs, its economic weight may be declining, but there is one front in which it is in the avant-garde. It has proven capable of constantly rethinking and interrogating its multiple pasts to produce an ever deeper and inclusive living history. Israel's politically engaged and scorched artists have been attracted to this aspect of European life as they seek to rediscover their European Jewish roots and also retrieve the idealism of the original Zionist message. It is no coincidence that these artists have little, if any, following inside Israel itself. Their message is inaudible because it distorts all the established identity boxes of a bubble-land.

A friend who works in one of Tel Aviv's most important contemporary art galleries tells me that Israel's millionaires prefer to invest in works of art whose international market value is guaranteed to grow. They are not interested in the often anguished or bitterly ironical existential quests of their own Israeli artists who stand at the crossroads of past, present, and future. They are perceived as too local and not sufficiently "bling-bling" in their eyes in an epoch that praises to the sky the works of Jeff Koons and other business/artists.

Yael Bartana is one of the most powerful artists in this Israeli quest for historical meaning. Born in 1970, she now lives mainly in Amsterdam but also in Tel Aviv and is well known for her videos depicting Israel's admiration of heroic nationalism, a kind of spiritual secularism. In her eyes, this admiration is the other side of the coin of the long history of Jewish persecution. In her most recent and most famous work, Bartana has chosen to confront this nationalism head on by transferring it to the European country that has shared Israel's fascination with heroic nationalism while adding to it its own notion of "martyrology": Poland. The interaction between Poland and Israel is even more shocking when one remembers that Poland was the home to the most important Ashkenazi Jewish past before its tragic end in the Holocaust.

What could be more iconoclastic and provocative for an Israeli artist than to militate for the renaissance of a new Polish Judaism? Bartana has done just that with her project titled *And Europe Will Be Stunned*, a series of three videos describing the fictive birth and consolidation of a "Jewish Renaissance Movement in Poland" (JRMiP). This movement militates for the return of more than three million Jews to Poland in the lands of their ancestors.[4] The first video, *Mary Koszmary* (Dreams and Nightmares), made in 2007, features a young Polish politician (played by an actual young left-wing Polish politician) who makes an impassioned call in an empty stadium in Warsaw asking three million Jews to return to Poland, so as to enrich once again a Polish people depleted by its too great homogeneity. The second film, *Mury Wieza* (Wall and Tower), made in 2009, follows a group of young Israeli and Polish volunteers as they build a small fortified camp, just like those built in the early years of Jewish settlement in Palestine. Crucial detail: this camp with its small wooden house and observation tower is being built in Warsaw across the street from the official Polish monument commemorating the fighters of the Warsaw Ghetto. As the camp tower is finished, the young politician arrives to bring the movement's flag—the Polish eagle with the Star of David as its backdrop—to the new pioneers, who are busily studying Polish (just as their ancestors had learned Hebrew). In the third film, *Zamach* (Assassination), made in 2011, unknown culprits assassinate the Polish politician. The film follows the official commemoration with his widow, an Israeli, and other fictional Israeli dignitaries in attendance. To mourn their leader, the new Israeli-Polish people come together in front of the iconic People's Palace, Stalin's gift to the Polish people, to honor a man who incarnated the ideals of openness, tolerance, and creativity based on the encounter with the "other."

The three films Bartana shot in Warsaw are striking for their visual esthetics, which purposefully evoke the nationalist movements of the 1930s, be they Soviet or Zionist, including references to Leni Riefenstahl's filming of the Berlin 1936 Olympics. Powerful and generous words are pronounced during the memorial service, words meant to strike against the national autism and the egocentric gaze of all countries trapped in their own historical rhetoric. Bartana criticizes precisely an Israel that has abandoned its earlier modesty to favor its own autistic national certitudes. The last sentences of her manifesto stand out as so many critiques to its new type of nationalism:

> With one religion, we cannot listen
> With one color, we cannot see
> With one culture, we cannot feel
> Without you we can't even remember
> Join us and Europe will be stunned.
> (Jewish Renaissance Movement in Poland)[5]

The significance of Bartana's work of art was further highlighted by the place where it was presented. Bartana's triptych did not constitute Israel's official presentation at the Venice Biennale in 2011, even though Israel in the past always took pride in promoting its avant-garde art. But in this case it refused to host Bartana. She was instead sponsored and financed by Poland in its Venice pavilion, the first time a foreign artist was presented in the Polish context. Bartana's message was equally applicable to Poland, where the conservative camp around the surviving Kaczynski twin perpetuates its own autistic vision built on a frozen historical memory. By welcoming Bartana in their pavilion, Poland's current cultural elites wanted to show their desire to open up their country to the world. What better way to do so than by daring to show a film in which a politician asks three million Jews to come back in order to create a new type of pluralist society? Bartana asks herself the question: Shouldn't Israel be doing the same thing? And she leaves us with an unanswered interrogation. Does the assassination of the Polish leader mark the end of a dream or the beginning of a movement?[6]

I had the chance to see the three films in Venice. Inside the white Art Deco pavilion with "Polonia" sculpted on the façade, the public plunged in total darkness was transported to the very heart of this fiction/hope. Yael Bartana has produced a great work of art. As an almost inevitable consequence, the international press did not mention the Polish pavilion in the stream of articles that accompanied the Biennale's inauguration. The topic was too sensitive and much too complex, combining as it did a multitude of classical references, the search for the purity of origins with which to denounce the nationalist excesses of the present. The use of a double Polish-Israeli dialogue that went against the clichés of both camps, and above all the reference to the old universal values of a humanist past in the name of coexistence with the "other," do not correspond to the ironical and jaded stances of most contemporary art. By taking the movement's manifesto, the visitor became an actor/participant of a fictional movement based on very real values.

The Israeli Pavilion was close by, and it was honoring another Israeli artist, Sigalit Landau, whose work had already been presented at the 1997 Biennale. It was difficult not to conclude that the Israeli commissioners had chosen an artist from the classical Zionist mold to counteract Bartana's provocative and destabilizing work. In an interview filmed by "Arte Biennale You Tube 2011," Sigalit Landau confirmed this impression, for without ever mentioning Bartana's name, she seemed to counter each of her fellow artist's stands.[7] Landau stressed that "she lived in Israel," that she had not chosen to "run away," that she did not like "slogans and grandiose sentences," and that she much preferred to work with her country's "concrete materials": earth, water, and salt. And indeed, Landau had installed at the entrance of the Israeli pavilion an elaborate system of water pumps and pipes to underscore the importance of water in Israel's future. Inside, a fisherman's net that had been plunged into the Dead Sea for several days, and that had turned into a salt statue once it had been brought back up to the surface, incarnated all ecological threats. Landau had pushed the nondialogue with Bartana one step further by exhibiting a large photo of a pair of Israeli army boots also whitened and solidified by the salt of the Dead Sea, and placed on a snowy beach not far from the Polish city of Gdansk, officially to commemorate Solidarity, Europe's grand democratic movement. But no one was wearing those army boots. The cut between Poles and Israelis was meant to be final. In order to provide some hope for the future, Sigalit Landau in the interview evoked her next project: to build a symbolic bridge over the Dead Sea between Israel and Jordan so as to plead for regional peace. She seemed to be unaware that her project quite literally arched over the Palestinians of the West Bank, excluding them from such hopes. Her work thus seemed as autistic in its optimism and as selective in its hopes as the President's Conference. Small coincidence: the Israeli Pavilion had been inaugurated by Shimon Peres, and his official car with the biblical menorah as unique license plate, which I had spotted on Route 443 on my way to Jerusalem, had just deposited the president for his trip to Italy. I am not sure that Peres with his dream of a vast peaceful economic zone covering the entire Middle East still incarnates today's Israel, which is both planetary and closed in on itself.

Paradoxically the same nostalgia for a constructive Zionist past floated in the Biennale air, as if both artists, despite their very different outlooks, had intuited that Israel had moved beyond its roots and its original hopes. Bartana's provocative and powerful work of art sought to anchor the Israel of the future in the new values of an old Europe. Landau's far more banal works sought to anchor Israel instead in its transborder geographical ecology.

Past/Future: back to Israel's basic questionings. But behind these two very different readings, both of which in their own way try to pierce the Israeli bubble, one can find yet a third metaphor, this time one that is intra-Jewish and connects Israel and the Jewish world beyond the country's borders. One can define this metaphor as an annex to the bubble, but a strange annex that would make it lose its floating quality. A bubble tied down to the earth by a precarious anchoring. I am referring to the "tent of the Jewish People."

8

THE TENT

The aquarium, the bubble, and now the tent constitute a triptych of Israel's many faces. The tent is by far the most engaging reference, for it encompasses a population that neither lives in the country nor is its citizen: the rest of the Jewish world. During the years of triumphant Zionism, the world's Jews were simply defined, in implicitly derogatory terms, as the Diaspora. The term has now lost popularity in Israel's official circles, if only because Israel is far too present in the rest of the world, both in terms of its economic and political interests and in terms of the number of its citizens living abroad, to define itself uniquely inside its own (still unclear) borders. Moreover, Israel profits from what can be called an inverse irredentism by which many of the world Jews have become virtual Israeli citizens by their unflagging and enthusiastic support for every Israeli action. Their primary concern is to support the "home country," albeit one with a recent political pedigree, through thick and thin. In its own interest, Israel is thus obliged to include the Jewish world in a dwelling symbolically larger than the state. Hence the tent.

The tent is not a minor symbol in the Jewish tradition. The Jews who left Egypt at the time of the Exodus, tradition says, dwelled in tents during their forty years in the desert. The tent protects and reassures while being light and easily transportable. The Festival of Sukkot, which commemorates the fall harvest, also celebrates God's protection of the Jews during the

Exodus. The key symbol of this important religious holiday is the *Sukkah,* technically speaking not a tent but a boothlike open-air temporary construction covered with palm leaves in which Jews are expected to come together for the seven (eight outside Israel) days of the festival, to pray and to take their meals there as a family or as members of a given Jewish community. With the *Sukkah,* the pragmatic original function of the tent was turned into a powerful symbol of human precariousness before the elements and above all before God. By underscoring the social and economic precariousness of their occupiers, the tents set up in the summer of 2011 in Tel Aviv were the secular equivalent of this ancient tradition. When Jews refer to the "tent of the Jewish people," they seek to evoke a precarious context in which Jews remain cohesive. As a result, all those Jews who are not inside the tent will find themselves isolated and run the risk of succumbing to outside threats.

The metaphor of the tent thus fits perfectly an Israel that is both strong and threatened—a country that thinks of itself as united in front of the enemy and for whom each diasporic Jew is a soldier in its planetary combat. But therein lie the metaphor's problems. How big is this tent, and should it contain all the Jews? If not, which Jews qualify for admission? And are there "bad" Jews who by their behavior have deliberately put themselves outside the tent? Last but not least, who decides the answers to these crucial questions?

The room is full. The session "On Thin Ice: Criticism versus Loyalty in Israel-Diaspora relations" is one of the most sought-after at the 2011 President's Conference.[1] A duel at the highest level is about to take place. On one side: Jeremy Ben-Ami, the founder of "J Street," the pro-Israel and pro-peace American Jewish lobby, designed to counter the influence of the American Israel Public Affairs Committee (AIPAC), the well-established lobby close to the Likud Party. J Street wants to be the platform for the voices of all those American Jews who still consider the universal values of a democratic society to be primordial and who want to actively pursue a two-state solution beyond mere rhetoric. Most J Street supporters voted for Barack Obama in the American elections. And it is not a coincidence that George Soros, the millionaire philanthropist, who had never previously committed himself publicly to Jewish issues, preferring plane-tary causes instead, has become one of J Street's supporters. The Israeli situation must have become dire indeed, in his eyes, to elicit such help. The movement has expanded beyond the United States with the birth of J Call in Europe. The Israel this move-ment supports is an Israel that seeks to be a normal country among others without any mystic-religious and idolatrous cult of the land. A country that can imagine living peacefully with its Palestinian neighbors: in other words, with a Jewish tent that can be pitched in an international camping site.

On the other side: Daniel Dayan, president of the Yesha Coun-cil, a former CEO of technological firms. Dayan is the chairman and spokesman of a council that federates all the towns built on the other side of the Green Line, in what remain technically Palestinian lands. But for the Council, the Green Line no lon-ger exists and "Judea and Samaria" are and must remain fully Jewish lands. It is up to the Palestinians to move elsewhere, ei-ther in Ramallah or ideally to Jordan. To facilitate the daily lives of the settlers, Yesha has become their spokesman when it comes to their infrastructural needs: more roads, more water, and of course, more construction. In brief it is an ideal grass-roots representative organization, were it not for the fact that its blades of grass grow on non-Israeli turf.

I have referred to the encounter as a duel between two major protagonists, but the session is actually meant to be a roundta-ble, one in which I also participate as a European Jewish voice, not exactly the most powerful position in the room, since European Jews are perceived in such gatherings as a weak, divided, and historically negligible presence. Two other persons complete the roundtable: an American rabbi, president of the Union of Reform Judaism, and a political scientist, and friend, raised in a kibbutz and who has preserved intact all of the optimism of Israel's early years while continuing to believe that an Israeli-Palestinian peace remains possible.[2] It runs in the family: she is Amos Oz's daughter.

The three of us in reality are little more than intellectual extras, invited to ensure that the session did not focus only on J Street. In vain: the public had filled the room to listen to the man who "dared" criticize the democratically elected—as their camp never fails to underscore—Israeli leaders, on behalf of a peace no one really believes in. The President's Conference claims to address all issues, even those that are controversial. It could have been the place where one might have debated for or against Israel's settlements or government policy over the Palestinians, if only in East Jerusalem. No such discussion occurred, for the simple reason that these issues are no longer debated inside Israeli society. They have become the purview of highly committed nongovernmental organization activists, a noble but not representative minority, increasingly marginalized by the "concrete" (in both senses of the term) logic of the new settlements.

Because of the "thin ice" reference in the session title, the founder of J Street began the session by evoking the "iceberg" toward which the Israeli *Titanic* was heading if it continued its policies toward the Palestinians. If Israel wanted to survive as a democratic and Jewish state, it had to pursue a two-state solution as swiftly as possible. Ben-Ami felt the time had arrived for Jews around the world to show "tough love" for Israel, by criticizing it when necessary in order to prevent it from going astray. His words fell on deaf ears.

The spokesman for "Judea and Samaria" replied with a stroke of genius. Ignoring Ben-Ami's concerns, he launched himself into a moving evocation of the Jewish tent. A tent, he underscored, that could even include those who criticized Israel's political choices, provided they displayed *that love of Israel* that was the cornerstone of the Jewish people.[3] Without such a love for one's fellow Jews, no criticism was valid. For the spokesman from "Judea and Samaria," it went without saying that Judge Goldstone, who had directed the United Nations' enquiry into the Israeli army's operation Cast Lead in Gaza in 2009, was clearly outside the tent, because his findings had helped Hamas. J Street's founder instead, according to Dayan, had *at first* belonged inside the tent. But Ben-Ami had lost his place inside when he had tried to convince American congresspersons not to follow automatically all of AIPAC's positions, so as to give the international community's peace proposals a chance.

Dayan then proceeded to list all the values that had made the Jewish people so special: love of one's neighbor, respect for the other, moderation in all statements, the will to remain united against all obstacles, solidarity, and the courage to remain loyal to one's principles. The problem with this list was that it could also be applied to many of the Jewish voices Dayan had defined as being outside the tent. And that is how Dayan, a Jew of Argentine origin and who had told us before the panel that his own brother was on the extreme left to the point of being almost anti-Israel, took it upon himself to exclude Ben-Ami, whose own father had been a member of the Irgun, the right-wing Zionist terrorist group responsible for attacks against the British during the Mandate period. It would be difficult to find a more perfect example of the intertwined emotional complexity of Jewish links and pedigrees in the making of incompatible political ideologies.

Thanks to Dayan's intervention, the road was wide open for the rabbi to elaborate on the biblical warning against "fratricidal wars" in a moderate speech that did not address any political issue. The Israeli political scientist stressed that in the Jewish world had indeed come closer together, compared to when she was growing up in a kibbutz when European and American Jews seemed very distant relatives indeed. Now we had all become cousins. My reflections on the incompatibility of the Israeli "never again to us" and the European "never again" were not even judged to be polemical. They were ignored in a context that considered all "things European" as utterly irrelevant.[4]

Reassured and comforted by the reference to the Jewish tent, the public, composed mainly of Israeli officials and Jewish community leaders from around the world, lashed out against Ben-Ami with all the nuance of a crowd in a Roman circus. It was clear from the general mood that the Diaspora had only one purpose: to behave properly by not pronouncing any criticisms and to follow the Israeli government's political line. The Jewish tent with its millennial existential pedigree had all of a sudden become little more than a private political club with its own admissions policies. One could no longer dissociate "Judea and Samaria" from Green Line Israel without immediately falling into the definitional trap not only of lacking "the love of Israel" but, far worse, of being an "Israel-hater." The great French political leader Georges Clemenceau, under whose rule France won World War I, used to say that one could not pick and choose different phases in the French Revolution. It had to be taken lock, stock, and barrel and treated as an indivisible "bloc." Those who subscribe to Daniel Dayan's definition of the Jewish tent adhere to the same line of reasoning. Israel is also a "bloc" and one cannot divide it into legitimate and illegitimate land without running the risk of abetting the enemies outside. Dayan's ukases from "Judea and Samaria," whether as verses from a new secular Bible or as pronouncements from a religious Committee for Public Safety, carried the session almost unanimously, with only a few souls left skating on thin ice.

During the summer of 2011, three events gave greater resonance to this debate. Jeremy Ben-Ami published a book titled *A New Voice for Israel* as a plea for J Street and the two-state solution.[5] He received bitter critiques from most establishment Jews, even those who in theory accepted the existence of a Palestinian state. Others, more to the right, even accused Ben-Ami and J Street of being liars and traitors to the Israeli cause.[6] On the Yesha side, Daniel Dayan, to ensure that the tent movement not be co-opted by those who might be "soft" on peace and dialogue, paid a well-advertised visit to the protesters in Tel Aviv to convey his support for the movement. He was warmly received. In another brilliant move, he told those in the tents that he understood their economic problems because young couples in "Judea and Samaria" shared them. They too needed better and cheaper lodgings and were suffering from the building freezes.[7] And he was not being entirely untruthful when one realizes that many residents of these contested settlements are not ultrareligious and moved there simply because the housing was significantly cheaper.

But this type of reasoning raises another historical specter. If the settlements in the occupied territories no longer derive their legitimacy exclusively from the biblical "fact" that God gave this land to His Chosen people, and if they are not really vital for security reasons, given Israel's highly sophisticated military defenses—then what other reasons can be brought to the fore? If they exist to allow Israelis to live in better conditions with more room at a lesser cost, this points inexorably, according to some Israeli journalists, toward an interpretation based on the logic of lebensraum.[8]

Nor could Ben-Ami in his struggle count on the support of Palestinians on the other side of the divide. Sari Nusseibeh, a prestigious intellectual who has presided for years over Al Quds University in Jerusalem, remained quite skeptical regarding J Street's power to change things. In his opinion there was no way the liberal group could take on AIPAC in Washington. As a result, Ben-Ami's book did not resound with any "new voice" but sounded increasingly like a last call without a future. If Israel continued to hang on to the occupied territories, according to Nusseibeh, sooner or later the only possible outcome would be either a confederation or a binational state.[9] Either way, it would spell the end of a Jewish and democratic state favored by the vast majority of the Jewish people. As an interesting parallel, one should note that Dayan's international visibility has grown markedly in the last year. He is now presented by some journalists in the American press as a moderate "pragmatist." And in July 2012, the *New York Times* published an op-ed of his in which he calmly announced that "Israel's settlers are here to stay," effectively burying any two-state solution.[10]

Israel's most conservative political camp has thus transformed the "tent of the Jewish people" into a closed setting, a virtual bunker. What has been lost in the process is the very essence of the biblical tent: its mobility, modesty, and fragility.

Another session of the President's Conference drew an even larger crowd, with people standing on the sides. Its title: "Conversion: Who Keeps the Gate for the Jewish Nation?"[11] The stakes were even larger than the Israeli-Palestinian conflict—and far more explosive, because they pitted different currents of Judaism and of the Jewish State against each other. The very reference to the "Jewish Nation" was far from neutral. Napoleon banned it from the French context, and the idea of Jews becoming citizens "like everyone else" was shared thereafter by

Western Europe and the Hapsburg Empire until the collapse of that order after World War I. The notion of the Jewish Nation, however, continued to exist in Eastern Europe and in pre-revolutionary Russia, and it was in these lands that Zionism took off as a historical movement. The title of the roundtable gave this concept a new life, because the "Jewish Nation" extends well beyond Israel's own boundaries. In order to emigrate to Israel and to benefit from the Law of Return, with all its attendant political rights, social obligations, and economic benefits, one has to be Jewish. But who holds the *imprimatur,* the ultimate decision-making power, to declare that someone is a "Jew"? Who can enter the Jewish religious tent? And who is left outside?

This is not just a theoretical question; it is a vital issue for Israel. A considerable number of former Soviet Jews with a Jewish father but a non-Jewish mother were accepted by Israel as citizens. Yet their families discovered subsequently, much to their shock, that the sons could not be buried in the Jewish cemeteries of the state, even when they had died as soldiers on the front. The rabbinical authorities simply did not recognize them as Jews. How can one solve this thorny issue in a country that recognizes no separation between synagogue and state? Is the religious tent as closed as the political tent?

These key issues were so vital to Israel's future that the most important political actors of the state chose to come in person to participate in the roundtable to plead their respective causes: the minister of justice, Yakov Ne'eman; the president of the Jewish Agency, Natan Sharansky; and the minister of the interior, Eli Yshai. Taken together, they represented Israel's three new identities. Ne'eman, the minister of justice, is a Sabra with Polish origins who comes from the nationalist religious camp, a former business lawyer with a somewhat controversial economic past, and equally controversial legal stands (with respect to the rule of law in Israel) when he pleaded for the recognition of religious tribunals in the handling of civil cases.[12] Sharansky, a former symbol of Soviet dissidence, heads the Jewish Agency, which quite simply created the Jewish state with a very secular orientation, in a manner not entirely different from the way the Communist Party created the Soviet Union. In both cases sheer political voluntarism and a concomitant dislike of religious institutions and judicial power, traits whose origins lay in the French Revolution, led to the creation of the two states. Sharansky on this count is very much the heir of both the Soviet and the secular Zionist pedigree. The minister of the interior, Eli Yshai, is the son of Moroccan Jews and was named as the head of the ultrareligious Sephardic Party "Shas," after its previous leaders were charged with corruption; he is also very close to Israel's chief Sephardi rabbi. Yshai occupies a key political position thanks to Israel's system of absolute political representation. Shas's votes were vital for Netanyahu's government coalition: as a result Shas was able to demand and obtained one of the key ministries. But the thinly disguised scorn with which Ne'eman and Sharansky contemplated their colleague spoke wonders about Israel's different political pedigrees. Yshai was not just religiously "black" but was above all Sephardic, and thus different. No longer present at the table were two of the founding legal currents of the Israeli state: the German tradition of the Rechtsstaat and the British tradition of the rule of law, both incarnated by a now-embattled Supreme Court that is losing ground to the other two constitutive legal strands: the rabbinical tradition and the intricacies of Ottoman law, used when convenient for land registration in the political agenda of the Netanyahu government inside the Knesset.[13]

The roundtable was completed by an American-Israeli female rabbi, president of Israel's conservative rabbinical association (not recognized by the two chief rabbinates), the only one besides liberal Jews that ordains women as rabbis; an American rabbi, president of the Central Conference of American rabbis, a nonorthodox conservative Jewish group; and an ultraorthodox policy researcher. The rabbi who was supposed to represent the Ashkenazi orthodox establishment had called in sick at the last minute, most probably because he did not want to sit at the same table with nonorthodox rabbis and a female rabbi to boot. Someone in the public spoke on his behalf during the question and answer session.

Compared to the political tent, the religious tent is paradoxically far more open, because anyone who has a Jewish mother is unquestionably Jewish both in religious terms and in belonging to the Jewish peoplehood, unless he or she has officially converted to another religion. It does not matter if such a person is an orthodox, an atheist, or a liberal Jew. If your mother is Jewish, no one can contest your right to belong to the tribe. That is why no Israeli government has ever questioned the legitimacy of such ultraorthodox Jews belonging to the Hungarian Satmar or the Lithuanian Neturei Karteh communities. Both refused to go along with Rav Kook's compromise and continue to hold anti-Zionist positions because for them a Jewish state will come about only by God's will at the end of the messianic times. All human anticipation of this event is pure blasphemy. These Jews have lived in Jerusalem since the eighteenth century and surely prayed in the first Hurva Synagogue. Their local pedigree predates Zionism by almost two centuries. And no one would ever dream of asking them to leave Israel, even though Neturei Karteh openly sided with the Palestinian cause (some of their representatives were photographed with Arafat during his terrorist phase, well before the Oslo accords) because they considered the state to be illegitimate. They even sent a delegation to Tehran for the Holocaust conference sponsored by President Ahmadinejad. They went to testify to the historical reality of the horror. As a result the Iranian president soft-pedaled his previous denial of the Holocaust's existence and declared that he was "simply" anti-Zionist and not antisemitic. Israeli leaders do not fear these thousands of ultraorthodox anti-Zionists. The current Israeli leadership finds Jeremy Ben-Ami far more problematic, because J Street listens to the international siren songs as Israel tries to navigate between the Scylla of the Green Line and the Charybdis of the occupation.

The roundtable was not set up to comment on the offspring of Jewish mothers, however strange or iconoclastic they might be. It was meant to address those who only had a Jewish father, and who could be Jewish only if they converted to Judaism. Officially only "one gate" was mentioned on this count, but in reality there is more than one port of entry, hence the conflict. It would be suicidal for Israel to alienate all those liberal and conservative American Jews who constitute the vast majority of American Jewry and who have been the most active supporters of the state, even in financial terms. Their conversions are not, however, recognized by the orthodox, who control the Israeli definition of who is a Jew, but who constitute only 10 to 15 percent of American Jewry.

As a result, Jews of all religious stripes, and some do not even have stripes, all live inside the Jewish tent, thanks to a Jesuitical (if one can pardon the expression) compromise. There can be, strictly speaking, no true accord between a state whose criteria for being Jewish were deliberately defined by ricochet against the Nazi Nuremberg laws (one Jewish grandparent), and different Jewish religious denominations, one of which (the orthodox) does not even recognize the existence of the others. And yet the Jewish world seems to muddle through. The religious tent is vast, and visibly no sound is loud enough to reach all of its nooks and crannies. One can therefore remain deaf to the demands of the others, and in this case indifference, even when it is hostile, remains the best guarantee for coexistence. Besides, for the really very complicated cases there is one last resort, a civil marriage in Cyprus (Israel has no civil marriage), a solution Israelis share with their northern neighbors, the Lebanese, when Christian and Muslim want to intermarry.

The roundtable participants thus reflected the contradictions of this nearly catchall tent. And in so doing, they managed to produce one fascinating oxymoron after another, each spanning centuries, when not millennia. First prize went to the minister of the interior, who was not actually scheduled to participate in the roundtable but had insisted at the last minute on making a quick appearance, TV cameras in tow, to have us benefit from his insightful perspectives. He spoke in Hebrew, for we were not his real audience. He was addressing his fellow Sephardic ultraorthodox, which comprise Israel's "Jewish street," and this made what he had to say even more alarming.

In a brief presentation, the minister announced that conversions were not at all the order of the day, except for some very rare exceptions. His reasons: ever since scientists had isolated *the Jewish gene,* it had been "proven" that a child born of a Jewish mother possessed it whereas a child born of a non-Jewish mother did not have it. And then, wonder of wonders, in order to remain faithful to the precepts of Jewish Law, the minister was quick to point out that there was an exception to this "scientific" rule: the case of the Cohannim, those Jews who claimed by their name to descend from the most prestigious tribe and caste because it provided the Temple priests. Miracle of miracles, in this case, the minister announced, the Jewish gene was transmitted by the father, because the Torah stipulates that one is a "Cohen" through one's father.

I know that this genetic reference stems from a much more complex debate. Scientists have not found *the Jewish gene,* but a series of genetic rapprochements among Jews coming from the four corners of the world, and this would confirm at least a partial common origin. Such a discovery is not surprising, given the fact that in their long history the Jews never ceased to move around while continuing to marry fellow Jews. Besides, because this type of genetic analysis is most often carried out on mitochondrial DNA, which is transmitted by mothers to their children, the maternal X genes are those whose continuum can be traced most easily in any genealogical research. In the case of the Cohannim study, the Y genes that the father transmits to his sons were used instead, and the results did show an interesting correlation among "Cohens," whether they came from the Sephardic Jews of Arab lands or the Ashkenazi Jews of Eastern Europe. But these are genetic correlations: no serious scientist has ever formally and openly evoked the existence of a specific *Jewish gene*.[14] Regardless of the statistical and scientific validity of some of these claims and counterclaims, what counts here is that the minister of the interior chose to mix and match parallel studies to suit his political ideological ends.

Furthermore, there are also political stakes to this debate: Israel's legitimacy as a state among others. For many Israelis there was an imperative need to counter the view that the Jews were an "invented" people, as one left-wing Israeli, Shlomo Sand, claimed.[15] Even if it were true and the Jews had invented their pedigree, as Sand claims, they would have behaved exactly like every other country. Historians well know that all nations in the nineteenth century went about inventing ancient pedigrees for themselves, whether among the heroes of the Trojan war, in Teutonic forests, or in other mythologies. The Jews on this front would be like every other people. In Israel's case, however, such speculation concerning the origins of the nation constitutes a direct attack against its right to exist. Among the reasons invoked in the Arab-Muslim world and by many Palestinians to affirm that the Israelis have no right to any Palestinian land, the most important is the claim that the Jews were never a people but are a mixture of different ethnic groups who converted in different historical periods to Judaism as a religion. In this reading, the Palestinians would be the true heirs of the biblical Jews, a people who converted first to Christianity before becoming in its vast majority Muslim with the advent of Islam. Hence, the Palestinian right and desire to expel from their legitimate lands the "false Jews," who thanks to their Zionist ideology pretend to be returning to their ancestral lands. For many Arabs, Jews are thus impostors. Genetic research on the Jewish people thus marks an attempt to counter this claim of Jewish nonbelonging on the contested land of Israel.

But as is always the case when one tries to combine science, identity, and politics, unpredictable and disturbing outcomes are the most likely result. Some people claim that a "Jewish gene" has also been found among the Pashtun tribes of Afghanistan—the tribes that brought forth the Taliban and against which the West has been fighting since 9/11—even claiming that they might be the famous lost tribes.[16] Were that the case, the specter of the extremes coming together would be confirmed, via the fake Russian-created (but based on an earlier French original) Protocols of Zion. The "evil" Jews would be back as those behind all the chaos of the world—and of course, once again, Europe and the West would foot the bill.

Such genetic games are too dangerous to play with, and of all peoples, the Jews are those who stand to lose most. It is not a coincidence if, after World War II and the Holocaust, postwar Europe's founding fathers were very explicit with the creation of the Council of Europe in stipulating that no country could define its identity and that of its citizens in either ethnic or religious terms. Israel is not in Europe, and it has never considered itself bound by such a European "never again." Its raison d'être was to be the place where the Jews were in the safety of their own homeland.[17]

And this is how Israel's minister of the interior could hold forth in front of his "Jewish Street" with statements based on such a false understanding of genetic principles, in the name of a blatant religious-racial identity, without incurring the least legal sanction. We had clearly left the realm of boisterous political debate for the murky waters of unsavory and dangerous concepts.

One could hear a few ironic murmurs here and there in the conference room after the minister's speech. Fearing that the interpreter might have missed some nuances as I listened to the minister through my earphones, I turned to my neighbors, all Israelis, and repeated what I had heard. They reassured me (not exactly the right term) that he had indeed made those pronouncements, and then they proceeded to laugh. In their eyes we had all experienced one more proof of just how idiotically obscurantist Israel's Shas Party could be—and by ricochet the Netanyahu government for having chosen it as a political ally. But none of my interlocutors seemed aware of or even worried by the democratic and philosophical implications of what had just been said . . . as if we had just been privy to a little political game. Period.

I am shocked. How can Israeli elites have so isolated themselves in their bubble to the point of not understanding that it was a state *minister,* and not an eccentric buffoon, who has just spoken in a language worthy of the worst racist logic? *The Jewish gene*: the mere idea evokes the Leipzig Institute for the Study of Races and Peoples in 1936, but an institute that would have been enriched by the genetic follies of Lysenko. But what is most remarkable is that all of this pseudoscientific banter is taking place in the same conference where Nobel laureates in scientific and economic fields participate in other roundtables with perfectly rational and universal arguments, considered as self-evident by the same public.

An international conference with its intellectual Smorgas-bords is being held inside the Jewish tent, but the tent itself has its own atmospheric pressure and oxygen levels. Israelis must possess lungs endowed with alternative currents, lungs that allow them to breathe equally well in both worlds, where others instead risk either giggly euphoria due to too much oxygen or suffocation linked to its absence. The alternative is somewhat stark: they may be endowed with schizophrenic brains, the tent and the outside world cohabiting inside the same person to suit his or her needs or perspective. It is as if those who live inside the tent were able in all impunity to resurrect a genetic "Jewrassic Park" while passing it off as a postmodernist novelty. Is this a miracle, a nightmare, or simply a political comedy?

Sharansky smiles. In a few succinct and powerful sentences he brings the roundtable back to the logic of political power and Israel's *raison d'état*. In his view, the Jewish Agency must be the final arbiter of any conversion, because it decides who can immigrate to Israel on the basis of the Law of Return, thus opening the way to all state benefits. We have been catapulted back into classical Zionism. An ultraorthodox researcher tries to find an interesting compromise (especially given his religious beliefs) between the two ministers. He makes the case for a secular Israeli naturalization process, one based on a cultural knowledge of Jewish and Israeli history. This secular naturalization would put an end to the double hypocrisy of having rabbis bend religious precepts to convert atheists or those who have no intention of following Jewish laws, and having these secular Jews hide their identities in order to be converted by orthodox rabbis.[18] The researcher's idea is perfectly logical and based on the purity of intentions. But no one seems interested, for the stakes of this entire conversion debate are far from rational. It goes to the core of electoral politics and the symbols of power.

The minister of justice did not mince his words. Immigrant workers and political refugees from Africa were his greatest preoccupation, without forgetting all those former Soviet soldiers who were denied burial in Jewish cemeteries by the orthodox rabbinical gatekeepers. In brief, how could one block the former and facilitate the integration of the latter? What international cooperation should Israel envisage to deal with the non-Jews on its territory? I am somewhat relieved. Clearly the justice minister was thinking within the familiar box of national prerogatives. I do not like his conservative understanding of identity and citizenship, but at least his categories are within the mainstream of our increasingly restrictive nationalist epoch. Israel is not that different after all. . . .

The roundtable presentations ended with the very rational and reassuring presentations of the American rabbis, who explained their respective conversion processes based on an intensive study of the founding texts. Their approach had a Protestant-like ethical conviction reminiscent of the Wissenschaft des Judentums, the scientific study of Judaism pioneered by German Jews in the mid-nineteenth century. This discipline, based on the use of comparative sources studied in a critical light and pioneered at the same time for Christian sources as well, is still missing within Islam. The American rabbis sounded like late nineteenth-century neo-Kantians, whose most famous Jewish philosopher was Hermann Cohen. It was as though the horrors of the twentieth century had never taken place. Despite its massive East European origins, American Judaism is the inheritor of the German Jewish tradition (which may itself be slowly coming back to life with the arrival of Russian Jews in Germany): American Jews believe in the possibility of reconciling religion with humanistic progress.

An acerbic remark by the minister of justice brought us back to the Israeli setting. Turning toward the woman rabbi, he commented sarcastically that she would do better to worry about the thousands of American Jews who were abandoning Judaism to intermarry rather than piously shepherd a few converts into the Jewish people.

And then came the final surprise. At the official end of the roundtable, the moderator gave the floor (as had been visibly arranged beforehand) to a representative of the Ashkenazi chief rabbinate. The man made no reference to genetics, misunderstood or real, but chose instead to concentrate his comments on what could be called, for lack of a better term, a historical deviation of genealogical geopolitics. He stood up and proclaimed that one could be Jewish only through strict obedience to Jewish Law, the Jewish people having been constituted at Sinai when they received the Tables of the Law. All those whose ancestors had not been physically present at Sinai could not really join the Jewish people, for they would denature by their presence the original Jews and above all the pact God had made with them at Sinai. For this orthodox rabbi, unlike for many progressive Jewish thinkers, Sinai with its covenant bore no relation for the Jewish people to the Geneva of Rousseau's social contract.[19]

A young man visibly from a modern orthodox current got up to contradict the Asheknazi rabbinate's spokesman. If the Jewish people were constituted at Sinai, he argued, then who were those who had fled from Egypt during the Exodus, and what about Abraham and Isaac? Were they not already Jews? His comment was met with total silence in the room, as though for the public the very future of the Jewish people hung on the answer.

The answer never came. The bell announced the end of the roundtable. The moderator thanked the participants. The public got up, thus bringing to an end a strange moment of collective hypnosis. Other sessions lay ahead: on the planetary economic crisis, on how to cope with neurological disorders, on ecological challenges, on the power of the media. The public rushed off to other parts of the tent in search of other role games.

A simple moment of identity thrills in a Jewish existential saga? A disturbing chapter in national politics? A Jewish polyphony based on a tribal dodecaphonic score? Or rather a frightening mirror of a Jewish tent desperately looking for mooring ropes, and finding them in a context that no longer seems to fit our Western references? The biblical burning bush has contaminated with its flames the democratic agora, and no one knows who will be the winner.

9

BETWEEN MEMORY AND MEMORY CHIP

The restaurant "Little Jerusalem" is situated off of Jaffa Road on Rav Kook Street next to Mea Shearim, Jerusalem's oldest ultraorthodox neighborhood. It is located in one of the most beautiful Ottoman houses built outside the Old City in the second half of the nineteenth century. The house is luminous and surrounded with its one balconied floor and magnificent terraced garden. Bought in the 1920s by Abraham Ticho, an important Viennese ophthalmologist and philanthropist, and his wife, Anna, a painter, the house served as Ticho's eye clinic where the good doctor received his patients from all social classes, including the Arab poor. The couple lived upstairs and led a busy social life entertaining their rich Arab neighbors, the British governing classes, Zionist political activists, clerics, and all types of intellectuals in what was a cosmopolitan hub. Anna willed the house to the city of Jerusalem upon her death in 1980, with the provision that it be turned into a cultural and music center. Today it is a quiet and elegant haven, including the ground-floor restaurant, a symbol of a distant past in a city that is catching up with the future. Right next to the house, a far taller luxurious residential building is being built. The Bubble has reached Jaffa Road.

On this summer evening, the restaurant's clients are all eating outside in the vast garden surrounded by old trees and sweet-smelling flowered plants. Only an aged ultraorthodox couple prefers to seek shelter inside. I am the guest of a German friend

whom I have known for decades. He has just arrived in Jerusalem to occupy an official function. As a very Catholic, very
European, very pro-Jewish, and very pro-Israel German, he is
beaming with joy to have moved to Jerusalem, a city that will be
his official home for several years. The fact that he is not Jewish
is important for me during this last evening of my Israeli stay. In
his presence, I feel I am returning to my usual atmospheric pressure, with a less anguished conversation, one that is less autistic,
because calmly open to the outside world. In Israel, everything,
including even the most spectacular aspects of its technological
avant-garde, seems to unfold on a razor's edge. And because
the sounds of the outside world are perceived as being ever
more hostile to Israel, this razor's edge has been placed (if one
can accept such a mixed metaphor) in a sound chamber. The
Jewish tent vibrates nowadays to its own sound waves. It is up
to the others to seize their frequency. My friend is committed
to such intent listening. He tells me that ever since he left Germany and Europe, with their morose contexts, their social hur-
dles, and their lack of a clear and strong political direction, he
has the impression of having taken a massive vitamin cure by
coming to Israel. Having left Europe's greyness behind, he tells
me he feels reborn, totally energized by Israel's stakes. In brief,
he too has moved.

We are sitting on the terrace. The guests who are dining next
to us al fresco look happy, at peace with themselves in a privileged context far from the world's noises. In a corner of the
garden under a pergola, several tables have been set up in a
square formation. Twenty guests are sitting around: two young
Lubavitch rabbis are in charge of the dinner, whose intent is to
bring the diners back to more serious religious practice. This is
a "how-to" lesson: the rabbis are explaining the Shabbat ritual.
Unlit Shabbat candles decorate the table next to covered bread
and wine, and an assortment of typical dishes. It is Thursday

and I imagine the two Lubavitchers are preparing their group for the Friday night meal. The lesson is taking place in English but the students are neither American nor British, not even Western European, for even the most assimilated younger Jews in these countries know something about Shabbat rituals. The dinner guests listen with the intensity of those who are to be initiated. I wonder whether they might not be recent arrivals from the former Soviet Union trying to find their long-lost roots and reintegrate a millennial past. The scene is both unusual and highly moving. Bread and wine: we are outside of time, at the very core of memory's transmission . . . but which memory and against which history?

Jerusalem, and with it all of Israel, contains too many clashing memories to celebrate concepts such as "in praise of difference," "culture's crossroads," and other fashionable mantras that Europe's beautiful cities and regions have come to revere in our peaceful times. Here instead there is virtually no mixing, little dialogue, and even less interreligious spirit. The memory of others does not add depth of field. On the contrary, it seems to subtract vital elements in one's own quest for legitimacy. Israel experiences itself at the first degree, its image glued to the mirror. Each group has its own memory, its own forgetfulness. The great Israeli poet Yehuda Amichai, in his last collection of poems, expressed perfectly the weight of these clashing memories:

And there are days when everything is sails and more sails
even though there's no sea in Jerusalem, not even a river.
Everything is sails: the flags, the prayer shawls, the black coats,
the monks' robes, the kaftans and kaffiehs,
young women's dresses and headdresses,
Torah mantles and prayer rugs, feelings that swell in the wind
and hopes that set them sailing in other directions.
. . . all of them sails in the splendid regatta

on the two seas of Jerusalem:
the sea of memory and the sea of forgetting.[1]

Israel, however, can also experience itself at the second degree, even the third degree, its "ears" wide open to capture the first sounds of the future. Not far from us, three men in their forties are sitting together under a tree. They are discussing in French the launching of a friend's start-up, their BlackBerrys poised on the table as a fourth piece of tableware. They are discussing the validity of his business plan. I hear term "memory chip" several times, but the rest is said so discreetly that no curious listener can seize the project's essence.

As I sit between the Lubavitch group and the French businessmen, I am struck by this strange stereophony. It encapsulates Israel's force and originality. Memory and memory chips, each in its respective sphere, belong to the same Jewish continuum. There is no need to worry about historical time in jumping happily from one to the other, whether it is inside the nonlinear circuits of a computer chip or inside a Talmudic page where the sages of all ages pursue a conversation with each other and the reader, without a care for the centuries that separate them.

Israel's strength derives precisely from this lack of history in the Greco-Roman sense of the term: history, which lies at the heart of Western civilization. Israel is not interested in conventional history's emphasis on origins, multicausal explanations, convergences, turning points, ironies, and tragedies. With no state past of its own in the last two millennia, Israel does not know how to cope with a history based on the interactions with neighboring peoples, whether allies or enemies. The historical method rooted in the Enlightenment and in nineteenth-century German historical tradition, with its precise and rational use of sources and of complementary and contradictory counterproofs, has remained an instrument and not an end in itself for Israel.

The country's self-proclaimed existential purpose was to pull the Jewish people out of other people's histories and to bring the Jews back into their own true past and destiny, out of their diasporic narratives.

It is thus no accident if in Israel Jewish history holds the high ground from within its own department, protected from any external influence, just like its sister, Jewish philosophy.[2] Jewish history and philosophy were taught to underscore Jewish uniqueness and not in a comparative light. It goes without saying that Israel has its share of professional historians and philosophers with world-class status. One should not, however, confuse a profession with an intellectual *topos* whose task it is to mold national debates, as has been the case in Europe from the nineteenth century up to the present.[3] The great American historian Yosef Hayim Yerushalmi perfectly expressed the identity tensions between "being Jewish" and "being a historian of the Jewish people" in his *Zakhor*.[4] In this book Yerushalmi explains how God and the entire Jewish tradition have always exhorted the Jewish people to "remember." No one ever asked them to offer a historical account (whether embellished or not) of their origins in the chronological and interactive sense of the term.

It is therefore not surprising to see that contemporary Israeli historians who focused on the political history of the State of Israel paid dearly for their work. I am referring to the "post-Zionist" historians whose writings began to appear in the 1980s when Israel's first archives opened. Because of their research in such a recent and still unsettled past, these historians have been marginalized inside an Israeli political context that could not integrate (even by countering them) their historical conclusions based on archival research. For these historians delved into such burning topics as the intellectual origins of the Israeli extreme nationalist right (inside European fascism) or the fate of the Arabs who were expelled from their villages and lands during the war of 1948 (did they flee following their leaders' exhortations—the official Israeli historical line—or was their eviction previously programmed?).[5] The current-day political implications of these sixty-year-old questions are such that one cannot really speak of a *historical* writing.

Grammatical syntax may lie at the core of this conceptual impasse. Zionism always considered the long diasporic period of the Jewish people as a period of more or less intense alienation. A long period in which verbs were either conjugated in the passive mode or remained intransitive, with the Jews never in a position to be the true protagonists of their actions. They were barely in charge of their lives and could influence their environment only occasionally and at best on the margin. The Holocaust provided absolute proof for such an interpretation of Jewish life in exile as based on existential powerlessness. Jews had only one role to play during the Holocaust: that of absolute victims. Saul Friedlander, in his monumental two-volume *Nazi Germany and the Jews,* made a point of integrating the actions, thoughts, and resistance efforts of the Jews as *actors* in a multifaceted historical understanding of the epoch. The premises of his book, and not the impeccable archival research that underpinned it, were deemed controversial, even unacceptable.[6]

Whether the Jews are truly actors in their own history is a conceptual problem that has yet to be resolved, above all in Israel. Paradoxically, the State of Israel, which by its birth should have brought about a fully sovereign Jewish people in full control of their destiny, was unable to, did not want to, or could not change the old "Diaspora" grammatical syntax based essentially on passive verbs. The Arab world, the Soviet Union, the Palestinians, the terrorists, the antisemites, those who advocated Third World causes, have all at one time or another taken on the role of politically dangerous subjects of constantly repeated passive verbs while Israel and the Jewish people remained the object (direct or indirect) of their guilty actions. Human Rights have thus become the last guilty avatar in this very long list. This was the opinion expressed by Jonathan Sacks, the chief rabbi of Great Britain in a plenary session of the President's Conference, when he presented "human rights" as the Western world's most recent and third antisemitic incarnation, after Christianity's Judeophobia and the scientific racism of the nineteenth century.[7] One can of course denature "human rights" and misuse the reference. However, to lump human rights, in itself a noble postwar principle, with two previous concepts that were fully invalidated in theological and scientific terms, seems to me an extremely dangerous idea, regardless of its rhetorical flourish.[8] Such a stance merely prolongs the tradition that considers the Jewish people to be powerless and at the mercy of the dominant weltanshauung in every historical epoch.

Since 1948, Israel has always thought of itself as a threatened state always obliged to react to the provocations of others and their desire to annihilate it. The country, on the other hand, never considers itself as an actor whose verbs (and military might) are responsible for actions of which others would become the objects. The victims of Israel's military or police actions, in this view, are simply collateral damage of aggressions perpetrated against the Jewish state by their own camp. One can deplore their deaths, but Israel never considers itself responsible, much less guilty, for their fate.[9]

The point here is not to negate the very real threats that continue to beset Israel, but to analyze the country's incapacity to change grammatical syntax. Israel is a strong and powerful country with many international ties. Its constantly repeated claims of weakness and fragility reflect a conceptual anomaly bordering on paranoia. And whoever thinks in an incomplete manner is bound to act problematically. On this count, Zionism has not transformed the existential status of the Jewish people. In many ways, it has aggravated it. Israel continues to see itself as an actor outside history.

This "nonhistory" has allowed the country to pursue its own destiny, one that allows Israel to fuse its biblical past with its globalized future. This path is self-sufficient and self-centered, with all "others" in the position of extras in the film of the Jewish people. Israel, unlike Europe, is a civilization without pre-biblical folklore. The Bible *is* Israel's folklore, for no external civilization with its priests, imams, or cultural middlemen brought biblical culture to the Jewish people from the *outside*. The Jewish people created the Bible with "its" own God. The millennial hatred of the Jews stems in great part from this undisputable fact: one rarely likes innovators or founders to whom one must remain beholden forever.

Only one other civilization resembles the Jews on this count, with its multimillennial past and its own self-centeredness also bordering on autism: China. One cannot account for the giant's current pride and militant nationalism without taking into account China's need to avenge its historical humiliation at the hands of the West. For nearly two centuries it too was unable to conjugate its verbs in the active mode in the wake of the Opium Wars when the British Empire overwhelmed the weakened, divided, and stagnant Chinese empire. [10] Unlike China, Israel did not just encounter early on the Greco-Roman sirens that underpinned the West. The very birth of the West under Christian rule robbed Israel of its own biblical memory. Today we would call this computer hacking: grabbing hold of someone else's memory, programming, and data without their consent and using them for one's own ends. Can one not see in Zionism and the return to religious orthodoxy, and even the intentions of the Temple Institute, a titanic effort (the very use of this adjective shows the extent to which I am beholden to Western culture) to claim back Jewish memory, to reprogram Jewish destiny, and to set up once again a fully Jewish search engine? Is it really by chance, in the psychoanalytical meaning of the term, if Israel is a world leader in computer security technologies as well as in the protection of memory chips?

Let us pursue this computer metaphor one step further. When one reformats a computer hard drive, one loses all data that was on the computer—unless it has been stored on another hard disk. Can one think of Jews outside Israel as being the equivalent of the external hard disc of the Jewish people? By constantly interacting with the others in whose midst they live, while also retaining a sense of history, can they provide a necessary anchor for a country that is losing both capabilities as it leaves the West?

I owe this intuition to my German friend's presence in Israel. Without him, it would have taken me far longer to reach such a conclusion, for want of perspective. He tells me that he is living temporarily in housing run by nuns of the German Borromean Order, and adds, laughing, that the food is heavy, because out of nostalgia for their country, they tend to serve German food with a lot of sausages. I can only smile: a convent behind thick walls in the heart of Jerusalem where würstel and sauerkraut triumph . . . how easy it is to forget all the "others" in the city, once one has entered the Israeli bubble.

All these "others" are virtually invisible and so silent amidst the intra-Jewish cacophony. The "German Colony" is one of Jerusalem's most elegant neighborhoods, now called with irony the "French Colony" because so many French Jews have bought apartments there as secondary residences that can easily be turned into primary homes "should things worsen in France." The neighborhood's German reference bears no relation to the arrival of German Jews fleeing Nazi Germany. The Germans referred to are *echte*, the descendants of Teutonic tribes; they belonged to the Teutonic order of the Templars, an order that settled in Jerusalem in the 1870s before Kaiser Wilhelm II's trip to the city. Hitler was interested in these German settlers, and along with Himmler he even envisaged exchanging "Jews of value" on their behalf to facilitate their return to the German motherland, but at the outbreak of World War II the settlers were deported to Australia by the British authorities.

I don't know how many Israelis have ever visited the Protestant Cemetery on Emek Refaim Street at the heart of the German Colony, a tree-lined haven of limpid silence. I never met any. During my last visit there, my only companions were a small group of Japanese tourists. Walking up and down its well-tended paths, I could only think that these dead souls were resting in exile in a world that no longer belonged to them: Templars, young wives of British pastors, travelers who died unexpectedly and whose bodies no family member cared to repatriate, German and British scholars of a colonized Islam, officers, children who died in young age. They were all buried in a Holy Land that no longer exists since it reverted back to a far more ancient holiness that was not theirs, leaving them as so many stranded silent witnesses of the tempests of a century whose contradictions are still with us.

The cemetery's heavy metal door is almost always closed. The opening hours are eccentric, and one must really want to visit the place to find its custodian. In other words, this cemetery's fate resembles perfectly the historical fate of Europe's Jewish cemeteries: marginal even when they were in the center of its cities, hidden behind heavy doors, practically inaccessible when they were not entirely off-limits, as in Eastern Europe under communism. But with a major difference: in Europe today, Jewish cemeteries have become "must" places to visit in any carefully organized itinerary of Jewish heritage, for Europe is now proud of and keen to publicize its many heritages and memories—especially with respect to the Jews. Will Israel one day also take into account all the other memories that surround it in such a vertiginous spiral of memory?

I must confess that in front of this Protestant cemetery I am seized by a strange sense of historical justice, as if for once things had been set aright. Thanks to Israel's existence, there now is one place on earth where the yearly calendar and the national holidays as well as life's rhythms are officially Jewish, where Time is conjugated in Jewish terms and where Jewish cemeteries are the rule rather than the exception. Israel as the vital protective space for a people who had been historically condemned, not to invisibility, but to too much visibility, if only through the compulsory wearing of highly visible distinguishing marks on their clothing in the Middle Ages—and of course in all the European countries under Nazi Germany's boot. The terrifying return of the yellow Star of David as a discriminatory symbol did more to destroy the Jewish understanding of civilization and progress than its ultimate conclusion in the death camps. History remains powerless in front of such a triumphant *and* tragic memory, whose continuity leaps over centuries.

My friend incarnates the very best of postwar Europe's ideals. He embraces an open and tolerant Catholicism, which considers Judaism as the vital pillar on which the Church must lean to avoid any pagan temptations (these are his words), a Catholicism that was revised by Vatican II and by the lessons of the Holocaust. His father was close to Konrad Adenauer, and he worked with Helmut Kohl; his childhood was molded by the Franco-German reconciliation. As a convinced democrat, he was very active in trying to inject democratic values in post-1989 Eastern Europe and the former Soviet Union. He thus incarnates Europe's loftiest spirit before the continent slipped into its current petty accounting squabbles. And now, toward the end of his career, he is eager to penetrate the Israeli riddle, full of the best intentions and with a far calmer, and definitely more indulgent, spirit than mine, for it is not his people. During our dinner, I am haunted by one single thought. Will he still have this same positive outlook and optimism in a year or two? Sooner or later he will have to confront Israel's hidden side, with its passive verbs and aggressive fears.

But can one present this hidden aspect without falling into a spiral of Israeli delegitimation, as the most stalwart defenders of the Jewish state claim? A state whose only truly active verbs accompanied the lightning victories of the Six Day War, a war whose long-term consequences are still unclear, for it is still too early to tell whether they were not Pyrrhic? The task is well nigh impossible.

Peter Kosminsky, a British filmmaker with Jewish origins, tried to do so in his television series *The Promise,* aired in Great Britain and subsequently in France in 2011. The film is a vast saga with two heroes: a British soldier sent to British Mandate Palestine during its last year in 1947–1948, a soldier who previously had belonged to the contingent that liberated Bergen-Belsen (and therefore knows about the tragic fate of the Jews), and his granddaughter, who discovers Israel and the Palestinian situation at the height of the Second Intifada, with its suicide bombings, while accompanying an Israeli friend who begins her military stint. The filmmaker was vehemently criticized by Britain's official Jewish circles and by Israeli representatives in the United Kingdom. They all considered it as the worst possible example of "anti-Israeli propaganda."[11] The Palestinian camp in the United Kingdom was instead more than surprised to see its past and present so faithfully represented in a television series.[12]

The film is above "guilty" (is that the appropriate word?) of transgressing well-established notions of time and perspective:

its angle and focal length do not correspond to the Israeli vision. Israel still vibrates to the mythical image of the birth of the Jewish state, as best exemplified in Otto Preminger's film *Exodus,* which was released in 1960, shortly before Adolf Eichmann's trial in Jerusalem. Kosminsky instead presents a pluralist version of the period, one that takes British, Arab, and Jewish perspectives into account, the latter no longer holding hegemony. No historical actor is spared. All bear their share of responsibility for the outcome. Everything Kosminsky describes actually took place, and it is most often Israel's new historians, so marginalized in their country's political debates, who furnished the documentary proof for the depicted events. Kosminsky's description of Israel then and now remains totally unacceptable for the vast majority of Israelis (and Jews) who adhere to a zero-sum reading of what has become an increasingly autistic spiral on both sides of the Israeli-Palestinian conflict. As a result, the terrorist Irgun replaces the moderate Haganah (officially the ancestor of the Israeli army); the "antisemitic" Britons become an army caught in an impossible struggle between two legitimate camps, and above all the undeserving victims of Jewish terrorist groups who dare to compare the British to the Nazis, they who fought at first single-handedly and bravely against Hitler's Germany. And an innocent and constantly powerless Palestinian population replaces an Arab leadership full of anti-Jewish hatred.

The film not only offers an anti-Preminger perspective. It conveys a message worthy of a Greek tragedy: blood begets blood. Terrorism (in both camps) can only breed more terrorism. Israelis and Palestinians are doubly guilty and innocent in a never-ending spiral. But for Kosminsky, it is above all the Israelis who have squandered the capital of support and sympathy the rest of the world had given them when Israel was born. The excesses of their pre-state terrorists and their reading of the world in 1948 prepared the setting for the misdeeds of the post-1967 occupation of the Palestinians and their own spiral of violence, including their terrorism.

Israeli subjects of violent verbs, direct complements of suffering Arabs, impersonal adjectives in both camps, possessive pronouns with too many antecedents: the grammatical loop closes in on itself, in a film that tries to replace memory with history, but a particularly astigmatic history because it is filmed through British eyes far from the Jewish epicenter. An impossible message for Israel to accept (to my surprise, none of my Israeli interlocutors had heard of the film) because the film presupposes that a historical debate can take place where for the time being only anguished certitudes exist in what is fast becoming the equivalent of the Hundred Years War.

The work of historians unfortunately will be of little use in overcoming this dilemma. There will be no archival wars: neither the Palestinians nor the surrounding Arab nations have any to speak of since 1948, and locating what exists is perceived as a Palestinian national priority.[13] If they exist, they are either closed or relate to religious courts. Israel is the only country in the region to have a documented past. No Jordanian, Egyptian, or Syrian document can contradict Israeli claims. I discover with great surprise that the Palestinians and the ultraorthodox Jews who fight each other with title deeds to the same houses in the Sheikh Jarrah section of East Jerusalem do so with documents that go back to Ottoman times, and that have been brought to light in the archives of Istanbul and Ankara. These archives are not much better, because Palestine at the time was a distant and poor province of a declining empire. This helps explain why both sides today accuse each other of presenting forged documents and equally forged proofs of sales. Their rival claims come up before Israel's Supreme Court, hardly the best venue for such disputes. And this is how the "lesson from East

Talpiot" is implemented with the triumph of injustice. Jews are allowed to settle in Jewish houses in East Jerusalem, whereas no Palestinian can recuperate even his own family's holdings in West Jerusalem. Added detail: these Arab houses fetch an even higher price in Israel's already very expensive but essentially modern housing market, because they are endowed with an Ottoman aura.

Power thus triumphs over nonhistory. Unfortunately, without the meticulous work of historians on both sides, postwar Europe has taught us, there can never be reconciliation. But for the time being those who speak of a possible Israeli-Palestinian reconciliation belong to a tiny minority.[14] For the others, one should take note that when people move, they often lose touch with their former neighbors, all the more so when they never had any friendly relations to start with. And even more so, when these neighbors have become, at an unconscious level, the ersatz of previous executioners and torturers whose descendants in the meantime have become friends.

After taking our orders, the waitress in the restaurant, a young Israeli university student, turns to my friend, who speaks perfect English but with a slight accent, and asks him where he comes from. For a fraction of a second he hesitates and then answers with a voice that has suddenly become very grave: "I am German." She turns toward him and with a charming smile, replies: "Oh, that's great, I would love to visit Berlin." She is beautiful and self-confident. Her black hair and dark eyes and caramel complexion denote North African Sephardic origins. The Germany that has accompanied her life is a placid and reunited country whose trendy capital, Berlin, shines with its cultural, musical, and artistic life, including nightlife. The young woman probably has friends who live there, given the significant numbers of Israelis who have chosen to move there for short, medium, or very long periods. Trendy Berlin: end of her German associations.

My friend is stunned. He had pronounced "I am German" with great effort and a hefty dose of embarrassment. He who lives with the weight of the past on his conscience has to face the fact: assuming they ever felt strongly about it, young Israelis have surmounted the old German reference. The Nazi past lies in the past. The country has changed enemies. The Arabs have replaced the Nazis, even if there is no common measure between the two. The Nazis had given top priority to the extermination of Europe's Jews in their political program. But once it was cured of its Nazi traits, the German enemy has become "normal" again in Israeli eyes. The Arab/Muslim enemy, on the other hand, is perceived as having a far more diffuse and pernicious anti-Jewish and anti-Israeli hatred, one that is far more unpredictable and therefore more difficult to eradicate.

I am not sure Israelis, and with them many Jews around the world, are aware of the paradox that underpins this twinning between yesterday's European enemies and today's Middle Eastern foes, in the name of their national raison d'être. Zionism was born on the margins of the Russian empire with the will to restore the dignity of a Jewish people who were vituperated and mistreated in a context of cyclical pogroms while facing the burden of constant state-induced discrimination. Without the Holocaust, one cannot affirm that Zionism would have carried the day and brought about the creation of the State of Israel, if only because of the anti-Zionist positions of most European and American Jewish elites. Europe's antisemitic tradition, crystallized in the Dreyfus Affair, which took place in a France heretofore considered as the epigone of freedom, in the brutality of the Russian empire, and later by the Nazi horror, furnished the vital arguments that legitimized the Zionist enterprise and transformed Israel's creation into a Western categorical imperative, even if it meant causing disarray in the local Arab populations. After the creation of the State of Israel this argument was further reinforced by the need to offer shelter to Jewish victims of persecution around the world, ending with the Jews of the former Soviet Union in what could be perceived as a return to the origins of Zionism (after the layered arrival of the North African Egyptian and Syrian Jews in the early 1950s, the Libyan in the 1960s, and finally the Ethiopian Jews in the 1980s).

I can well imagine the bitterness with which the Arab populations that now define themselves as Palestinian contemplate the ever growing and ever stronger ties that bind Israel to the former executioners and tormentors of the Jewish people, guilty in the past, as all of Europe, of latent and not so latent millennial antisemitism. Germany is considered today as Israel's best friend after the United States, and Russia as a new friendly power with its own intense ties to Israel's former Soviet population. In a Middle Eastern world where ancestral enemies remain just that—eternal enemies through ancestral hatreds that simply won't go away—in a context where Sunnis and Shiites have killed each other ever since the death of Muhammad, any rapid Western change in status from mortal enemy to friend is simply incomprehensible. Less than sixty years for Germany (and only twenty for the establishment of diplomatic relations in 1965), less than a century for Russia (and only twenty-five years for the Soviet Union)—these are time scales that in Arab/Muslim eyes implicitly weaken Israel's existential arguments, even though their legitimacy is uncontested in international terms. Such discordance in notions of time transcends the political realm to embrace far deeper cultural fractures with the Holocaust inevitably caught in the middle.

My German friend is an adoptive child of the Holocaust. Its black light has pointed the way in his life and guides his political choices as a German who seeks to build a better future. Negation, relativization, or simply the will not to consider the Holocaust as pertinent with respect to their own suffering have instead marked Arab attitudes toward this chapter of Jewish life. And this indifference to the Holocaust has grown over time. For the Arabs as a whole, past wrongs do not a right make.[15]

But what about today's Israelis? Do they still think of themselves as the children of the Holocaust? I am not so sure. I would be tempted to say that the Holocaust as a reference has just completed its first metahistorical cycle. First of all as a tragedy experienced by its survivors, who were not really listened to in the first years of Israel's creation, since in the eyes of the Israelis they had not made the right choice of moving to Palestine before it was too late.[16] Then as a moment of national pride during the Eichmann trial, for however small compared to the scale of the crimes, Eichmann's capture, condemnation and death sentence represented a moment of retribution. Finally: the historical commemoration of the Holocaust during the decade spanning its fiftieth and sixtieth anniversaries (1995–2005). This "return" of the Holocaust was marked by Israel's first encounter with the geographical places where the tragedy had unfolded, in the newly liberated lands of Eastern Europe after the fall of communism. This implied also meeting and coming to terms, not without difficulty, with the peoples of these lands, whose elders had actually witnessed the extermination of their Jewish neighbors (when they were not perceived as having abetted it). This historical moment of commemoration with *Jews and non-Jews,* coming together with clashing emotions to confront the Holocaust, has now come to an end. Ritualized encounters and educational programs continue, such as the teaching of the Holocaust in European high school curriculums.[17] Conversely, young Israelis make organized trips to Poland to see the death camps (trips now enlarged to include meetings with their young Polish peers in order to break antisemitic but also anti-Polish stereotypes). Tourism in "Yiddishland" and other cultural and artistic endeavors continue to flourish, thus bringing back the presence of the Jewish absence in Eastern Europe. All of these activities are becoming traditions in their own right, but they are inevitably routinized. There is no longer any need for courageous dialogue.

The Zeitgeist has moved on. One can wonder whether today the Holocaust has not sunk, once again, below the Israeli horizon. It will surely return, not unlike Halley's comet, in a more distant future, but in a different incarnation: as one of those key symbolic moments of an ever-longer ritualized and ahistorical Jewish *memory* and no longer as a *shared history,* which by definition thrives on a dialectical movement of constant readings and reinterpretations. The others in the Western world will continue to confront the Holocaust in an ongoing attempt to find answers that can be used as universal lessons. Israel, and with it most of the Jewish world, will probably want to bring the Holocaust back into its own Jewish ethnic fold, far from the world's madding crowd.

With its move into planetary cyberspace, Israel is transforming the Holocaust into an emergency kit to be carried in its delocalization. The number of Israelis for whom the Holocaust belonged to their own family's ancestral past is constantly decreasing. The vast majority of former Soviet immigrants came to Israel without the Holocaust in their family baggage. The same is true for those Sephardic Jews from North Africa, and even more so for those Jews coming from Turkey, Iran, and Yemen, not to mention those who came from Ethiopia. Furthermore, the Ashkenazi ultraorthodox, who in their vast majority did come from the Eastern European lands of near total extermination, have always surrounded the Holocaust with a wall of total silence, perceiving it as something shrouded in divine mystery, and certainly not as a moment that could be either understood or explained by human reason. As for those North and South American Jews who chose to settle in Israel, at times for reasons of manifest destiny linked to "Judea and Samaria," they are the descendants of the vast East European immigration of the turn of the twentieth century. Their families had left Europe well before the tragedy. Each of these groups thus possesses its own identity, its own future, and its own past it has chosen to transcend.

Given this context, the Holocaust is fast becoming a memory chip in the mental geography of Israel's new generations, a database that is always available but that no longer conditions, by its omnipresence, the country's programming. At Yad Vashem more than a decade ago, I remembered seeing young recruits in the Israeli army sitting cross-legged on the floor in front of a life-size reproduction of a street in the Warsaw ghetto, with the ghetto wall in the background. A guide was explaining to them the historical horror, and they were listening to him like well-behaved schoolchildren, in total silence. I had contemplated these young recruits for several long minutes. They incarnated so perfectly Israel's many faces: some were black, others were red-haired with freckles; some were blond with fair complexions, others were dark-haired with olive skin, while still others seemed particularly pale. One could not dream up of a better metaphor for the ingathering of all the Jewish diasporas . . . but this coming together had as a focal point, the pile of rifles they had left outside. The Second Intifada had not yet begun; no separation barrier prevented the Palestinians from entering Israel's cities, but the imprint of the ghetto, this time self-created, had already configured the mental geography of these youths who did not know and did not interact with any others.

I had evoked this scene on the spot with one of Yad Vashem's curators. Her reply was immediate: "We have all become Polish

Jews" she told me, exhibiting a sense of despair, for she could measure the irony of such a stance with respect to the original Zionist project. The Holocaust these army recruits were absorbing was detached from any historical reality. It had been channeled into an entire people's subconscious and transformed into a timeless emotional grid. Its commemoration could no longer serve as a moment of reconciliation between Israel and other countries, a moment that could have brought Israel closer to Europe by giving the Jewish state the sensation that it was no longer alone and alienated from the international community.

We are thus faced with a major historical cleavage whose consequences are primordial for both Israel and Europe. The disappearance of the historical Holocaust from the Israeli horizon is accompanying its move into its own identity orbit—at the very same time when Europe has understood the historical importance of the old (and new) Jewish presence as avant-garde symbols of its own pluralist modernity, with the Holocaust constituting the ultimate black abyss. Sad irony of history: from all over Europe, the number of requests from individuals seeking to have parents, great-grandparents or other close contacts honored with the title "Righteous" never ceases to grow. But this international recognition of the Jewish concept of righteousness as universal symbol of the loftiest human generosity is taking place when Israel is turning its back to such recognition by perceiving itself as a lone knight increasingly delegitimized and loathed by all. The result: on one hand, the syndrome of the amputated limb, whose absence/presence still evokes pain; on the other, a syndrome of a new life without the baggage of the past. And between the two, all the misunderstandings linked to a failed encounter between History and Memory.

One of the most striking examples of this failed encounter took place in 2001 when Yad Vashem took possession of nearly all the wall frescoes the Polish Jewish artist and author Bruno

Schulz had painted in 1942 for the children's room of a Nazi officer stationed in Drohobych, Schulz's native city. The frescoes, hidden behind thick coats of paint, had been discovered shortly before after nearly sixty years of oblivion. The Polish and Ukrainian authorities (Drohobych is now in Ukraine), had considered transforming the house of the Nazi officer into a cultural center that would pay tribute to the city's pluralist, including Jewish, past, and in so doing honor the memory of Bruno Schulz, who felt profoundly Jewish, Polish, and cosmopolitan.

Yad Vashem, claiming its moral right as the depository of the Jewish people's Holocaust past, took hold of the frescoes (literally in a fly-by-night operation that was compared to the freeing of Israeli hostages in the Ugandan capital of Entebbe in 1976) without asking the authorization of the Ukrainian government. A major controversy ensued between those (among whom many active Jews in the new Eastern Europe) who felt that Schulz's artistic patrimony should have remained in situ as a tribute to a lost Jewish world but also as a symbol of a pluralist future.

These voices were pitted against all those who considered Schulz's oeuvre above all as the creation of a Jew who worked almost literally as a slave at the behest of a Nazi officer, and therefore a work that would not have existed without the Holocaust. Schulz's frescoes in this reading epitomized the horror of Jewish suffering and death and therefore had to be repatriated as quickly as possible in the depository of Jewish Holocaust memory at Yad Vashem. This position was made clear by leading Israeli intellectuals who scoffed at any attempt to keep the frescoes in the Ukraine.[18] In the end a compromise was found between the upholders of the Jewish memory and the upholders of a future European pluralism. The frescoes were restored by Yad Vashem but they remain formally the property of the Ukrainian state, which officially has "lent" them to the Israeli institution.[19]

The truth behind the story is far more ambiguous. Israel considers itself as the sole depositary of Jewish memory, one that is not contaminated by external forces. Jewish history, with its inevitable interactions with other peoples, not to mention its ties to a Europe that has understood the importance of the Jewish contribution to its pedigree, can only be perceived as a secondary national pursuit, a minor intellectual vocation with respect to the memory needs of the Jewish state. My German friend does not know it, but his existential raison d'être is no longer compatible with that of an Israel that shuns all attempts to turn it into a normal nation among others, preferring to isolate itself in its own specificity.

It is late. Most dinner guests have left. The Lubavitch dinner hosts and their acolytes are long gone, the businessmen as well. Only the ultraorthodox couple inside with its heavy silences, and a few late diners who are savoring the sweet night air, are still there. My German friend and I step out onto Jaffa Road under a starlit sky: he to return to his convent, I to my hotel . . . when suddenly Jerusalem's new streetcar appears, seemingly out of nowhere. It advances in frightening silence, without passengers, its seats still wrapped in plastic. It is being tested, for the city's inhabitants must learn to factor in its presence on a Jaffa Road that has been totally transformed and cleared of all car traffic to accommodate it. The tram's stops must be synchronized with the traffic lights and in order to ensure a smooth circulation, the time it takes between stops must be carefully calculated. In brief, one must rationalize a traffic flow that has never known such mathematical precision. On both sides of Jaffa Road, people in cafés are enjoying their ice creams and drinks. A bit further down the road, the tram will turn left and begin the great descent toward the Damascus Gate before heading out to the city's other Jewish neighborhoods. It will then turn the seemingly impossible into a banal reality: by opening its doors to both Jewish and Arab residents of Jerusalem for a shared, even if short, trip together. Is it the beginning of a dream? Will its technological reality turn into a political optical illusion? Will it make history? No one knows. In eerie silence the tram moves on: ghost ship of an enigmatic future.

10

STARGATE

A circular portal, dating back several thousand years, planted in the middle of the Egyptian desert, on which are inscribed mysterious symbols all along its circumference, each pointing in a very specific direction. This is the key object in Roland Emmerich's 1994 film subsequently turned into several cult TV series under the name *Stargate*. In these intergalactic series, the portal, discovered by an archeologist, turns out to have been in the distant past a key communications instrument between Earthlings and other living beings on other distant planets. The archeologist, after having decrypted the portal's mechanism, realizes that it is still in working condition and can communicate with other portals across the galaxy. The portal becomes an ultrasecret military base because it allows Earthlings to communicate with other worlds and to protect the Earth from any intergalactic attack. The specialists who walk through the portal can, by choosing a given destination, be immediately transported into other civilizations and other time/spaces. Fortunately they always manage to find the right portal to bring them back safely to Earth, but only after having survived thrilling and dangerous encounters.

I must have seen the original *Stargate* television series with my children in the 1990s, for it suddenly pops up in my mind as I walk around the circular departure lounge of Ben-Gurion Airport. Can one think of the Israeli and Jewish travelers who use the airport as the equivalents of intergalactic travelers connecting different worlds to their *Eretz,* literally the "Land/ Earth" in Hebrew? Back home I look up the *Stargate* series and find the following definition:

> The Earth, a newcomer at the intergalactic level, often behaves like a bull in a china shop, by multiplying its awkwardness and turning upside down a previously established millennial order, but succeeding on the whole—and often at the very last minute—in improving the general situation thanks to its new outlook and thanks to the ingeniousness, humor, and pugnacity of its exploration teams.[1]

Replace "Earth" with Israel and "exploration teams" with traveling Israelis and Jews, and the match fits perfectly.

Thanks to the VIP service of the President's Conference, I was able to clear the police controls in less than fifteen minutes: a true record that leaves me with another time record on my hands: two hours before my flight. I use the hours to walk around the vast circular hall, best defined as a functional shopping mall with different corridors that take travelers to their respective gates. I think of the Israelis who are getting ready to depart as so many travelers about to cross the Stargate into other worlds. On the other side, they will find planets with other atmospheric pressures, other space/times, and above all, other preoccupations. And these other worlds will reinforce the Israeli conviction of being different and endowed with a special destiny. For the cities displayed on the screens are not simple geographical destinations. Each incarnates in Jewish terms either a spent past, a complex present, or a possible future . . . sometimes all three at once. None is neutral. All participate in the great passionate drama of Israel in motion, Israel in the world. Point the Stargate toward Moscow, Warsaw, Berlin, Amsterdam, Rome, London, Paris, Madrid, or Lisbon and glorious and tragic pasts appear, combined with fertile and at times ambiguous presents. Point it toward New York, Los Angeles, Buenos Aires, São Paulo, or Sidney and realms of ongoing hope light up. Point it toward Singapore, Bangalore, or Shanghai and an announced future pops up in the shape of a promising, but also deforming, mirror. If only Beirut, Baghdad, Damascus, Teheran, Cairo, Tunis, Tripoli, Casablanca, and Fez were announced, then the millennial Stargate would be complete.

As I meander in the vast hall, I am also struck by another comparison: I feel I am in the middle of a panoramic screen with 360-degree vision, the kind of screen that is used to replay Napoleonic Wars or Civil War battles or in more peaceful terms entire ecosystems—the Brazilian forest or the Antarctic—"as if you were there." And I am there. With only one international airport, all of Israel parades in front of me. I live a condensed version of all of my stays, of all of my experiences, of the country's past and future.

Clutching a handful of flyers, the man dressed in classic black and white with a flowing white beard and a large black hat paces in front of a white counter, behind which a large grey inscription spells "Lubavitch" (in English). He clearly knows how to attract lost Jews, for he has an uncanny ability to seize their gaze and to approach them with a large welcoming smile, even in such an improbable place full of rushed travelers. The position of his stand has certainly been chosen with great care. It is next to a large toy store. Those who enter it must have some link to children, otherwise they would not be buying toys: parents, uncles and aunts, grandparents, cousins, friends. They are the ideal targets for a Jewish lesson, because Judaism has been defined since time immemorial by its transmission to future generations. Its children must remain inside the Jewish tent for the Jewish people to survive, and they will only do so if they have a Jewish education. The cuddly toy or the Lego box should remind their buyers of this sacred duty, and the men in black are there to refresh memories. I follow the Rebbe in action. He never seems to give up. If no one comes toward him, he goes off to greet anyone who happens to walk by.

A short and squat man walks by wearing a pair of stretch pants and a blue T-shirt. It is hard not to notice him. He is a bodybuilder and clearly strutting: with his military gait, his Ray-Ban sunglasses perched on his suntanned forehead. It is impossible to guess his origins: Soviet, North African, from the Caucasus, European? They have all given way to a new entity, the sybaritic Sabra. His body, unlike that of the Rebbe, who thinks of his body as simply a divine vehicle for action, is clearly at the heart of his entire identity: the mirror others must contemplate. The bodybuilder walks by with his enlarged pectoral muscles, his taut biceps and triceps in full display, every single abdominal muscle sculpted to perfection, and all of this mass set off by a wasp's waist. I read the Internet address of his Tel Aviv club, in bold white letters on the back of his T-shirt. He walks by the Lubavitch counter, but his eyes do not meet those of the rabbi, whose back is turned to him: a double nongaze of indifference.

The bodybuilder heads not toward the toy store but toward the biggest sports store I have seen in my many years of airport travel. One can only compare it to Ali Baba's cavern. An impressive collection of tennis and badminton rackets stands next to one of the biggest selections of team shirts from the world's most important soccer clubs. Running shoes, sweatpants, and sweatshirts fill many aisles, next to all sorts of swimsuits and diving gear. Athletic supplements from pills to creams, muscle enhancers, pedometers, heart monitors, calorie counters stand next to the cash registers to be bought on the spur of the moment before the final checkout. The store contains everything one can possibly want to perpetuate the Greek ideal of the Olympic Games of yore—a tradition that was both proscribed and despised by classical Judaism.

Where does this need to display such a wild quantity of athletic goods come from? Does Israel possess so many Saturday athletes? I think back to the dialectic that prevailed in the late nineteenth century, pitting pale-faced religious Jews against athletic Jews who honed their muscles to better fend off antisemitic attacks and to counter stereotypes of stooped and weak diasporic Jews. A century later, might this dialectic still be valid, pitting the Rebbe against the bodybuilder? Or do they incarnate two sides of the same Israeli coin, one deliberately pale, the other deliberately suntanned, of a pacified identity in their common allegiance to the Israeli "www.'s?" I prefer the second alternative, with its stunning visual contrast. To each his life, with a minor caveat: have all these running shoes bridged the gap between the old wandering Jew and the new traveling Israeli? Inside, I notice an elderly ultraorthodox Jewish lady wearing a scarf over her wig, who is trying on a pair of canvas sneakers, surely to relieve the pain of her old feet . . .

I continue my panoramic tour. Next to the sports store, a highly predictable boutique selling mobile phones, high-tech goods, computers, tablets, and all sorts of musical gadgets welcomes the usual crowd, with one strange exception. Next to a stack of catalogs at the back of the store one can spot refrigerators, washers, and dryers: startling items one does not associate with duty-free items in sealed plastic bags. But that is what they are, despite their weight. Israeli travelers order them before traveling abroad, and when they return they have them delivered to their home without having to pay the import duties. This strange system dates back to the time when Israel was a poor socialist state with very few consumer items on the market and too few inhabitants to warrant the creation of its own appliance and car industries. Times have changed, but Israel never tried to catch up on this traditional industrial front. The country simply leapt over this mechanical phase to become a leading high-tech oasis. I am told it is even becoming a life-size testing ground with electric plugs along its highways for Renault's future electric car. And this is how the old duty-free system endures, underscoring one of Israel's greatest strengths, its ability to combine the best of different industrial epochs and historical times. Two young couples, availing themselves of their trip overseas, are ordering appliances for their home.

The tour continues. A boutique selling tourist souvenirs strikes me for the poverty of its shelves devoted to Christian objects: a few votive candles, some small vials containing water from the Jordan River; some olivewood crosses (without the sculpted Christ), and some colorful earthenware decorated with the Christian symbol of the fish—that is all. The rest of the store is full of Jewish items, earthenware inscribed with Jewish proverbs, small ritual objects, all sorts of Mezuzahs to hang outside the house door, in compliance with the biblical commandment to remember God and His Torah at all times, some wooden spice boxes for the conclusion of the Shabbat. Piles of loud-colored T-shirts with lettering that evokes all sorts of Jewish jokes or conveys an alarming sense of hubris—"Americans fear not! Tsahal is here to protect you"—complete the displays along with all sorts of Jewish cookbooks and joke books, each with its 100 ethnic and comic ways of being Jewish, brought home by Jewish tourists as proof that they have indeed participated in Israel's joyful ambiance. There is not a single Arab object in sight, no textile, no earthenware bauble. For those one had to have shopped in the eastern half of the Old City or in Akko. Ben-Gurion is the planetary airport of the Jewish world and its goal is to facilitate Jewishness. In the store I am struck by one last detail. The Christian customers look at the souvenirs they are buying as if they had already been turned into *ex voti*. No similar respect among the Jewish buyers: Jewish trinkets remain trinkets.

The bookstore nearby is full of books in Hebrew and children's books on how to learn the language. For the non-Hebrew reader, it is also a useful place to buy English translations of nonacademic literary and historical works. One striking note: very few books on the Holocaust and only by Israeli authors; no German or European accounts. The horror has become home-bound. Nor does one find many current affairs books. They are not relevant for a country that is constantly living on the razor's edge. Literature and poetry, instead, hold center stage, and it is no accident that Israeli writers are so well known around the world: their work is forced to address burning topics and trag-edies in a language that conveys both depth and uniqueness, and achieves a universality our fatigued and flat Western set-tings lack. The record store nearby focuses on Israeli music, rock, and pop songs, and also sells the country's top TV series and films to all the Israelis living abroad who are nostalgic for their culture and who want their children to grow up with it, so they can feel at ease when they return.

When I reach the corner with the fast-food stands, which juts out like a growth from the circular mall, I feel that some-thing is missing from the usual airport fare. But I have to circle the area twice before I realize what it is. There are no dimly lit pubs in the airport: those faithful hideouts for travelers who like to drink alcohol at all hours. Is this the final sociological proof of what is often claimed, namely, that Jews drink infinitely less than their Christian peers? The lack of pubs turns the food plaza into a far healthier looking spot, as if it had been spared life's problems to be drowned out in alcohol—perhaps because collective national problems have taken their place.

High-quality jewelry counters with precious stones, gold bracelets, pearls, and even diamonds fill the center of the circu-lar mall, right next to small stands that sell dates and sunflower seeds—as if there were a logical link between the diamond-hard heritage of the Jewish merchants of Antwerp and the softness of the sweet and plump dates dating back to the ancient biblical tradition. A crowd of ultraorthodox Jews moves back and forth between the two counters, clearly buying on both fronts. They seem to stand in unison with their long black silk frock coats, and they make me think, despite their beards, of young women of yore, because they tote with utmost care large hatboxes that protect their *Shtreimls,* the large fur hats worn on Shabbat. One has to have seen several of these men, both young and old, go through the security portals—their anxious eyes fixed on their precious boxes, lest much to their horror they be confused—to savor the sweet irony of this comparison and tradition.

"Tradition": an overused term, with an inescapable other connotation in the Jewish world. Is the boutique that sells little flowered dresses with lace collars and sleeves, along with dainty laced boots hearkening back to the 1900s, bell-shaped hats reminiscent of the roaring 1920s, and Art Nouveau Gallé-style lamps really surfing in all innocence on the wave of "retro" fashion? Or does it reflect a certain Israeli nostalgia for a lost world that was paradoxically easier, since without a state the Jewish people had no national responsibilities? Recreating such a world, even in an airport boutique, is hardly happenstance. I contemplate the clients inside: young Israeli women with their years of compulsory military service behind them who are touching the cute little dresses and trying on the boots, as if they were in search of a lost old-world femininity with its spell-binding scent.

Last stop in this circular odyssey: the elegant boutique that sells silver ritual objects, some in pure silver, judging from the price tags. The entire Jewish tradition is present on the shelves, from the silver hand "yad" used to read the Torah scrolls in the synagogue to the Seder Plates for Pesach, including fine silver Shabbat candlesticks and the predictable eight-candle Menorah for Hanukkah. These artisanal items are not necessarily beautiful: most are pompous in their heaviness and have nothing in common with the elegant ultramodern-design ritual pieces one can find in trendy boutiques, and even less with the splendid Jewish artifacts produced in Renaissance, Baroque, and eighteenth-century Europe, most of which have found their way into the ever-growing number of Jewish museums across the continent. Heavy as they may be, these ritual objects still symbolize the importance of Jewish ritual and convey a very moving sense of tradition, not unlike a heavy old aunt with a stiff gait. They make for imposing wedding presents when new Jewish households are created.

In this boutique my gaze falls on a most impressive object, given its size and symbolism: a silver version of the seven-armed menorah, as big and as tall as the golden one installed by the members of the Temple Institute on the steps leading to the Kotel. This silver version is for sale, but its hefty price is not visible since there is no price tag on it.

What an ironic setting: a life-size menorah for sale, standing in an airport concourse, and ready to leave Israel with whomever buys it—in a far more benign trip than that of the original, which accompanied the Jewish contingents who were taken to Rome as slaves after the destruction of the Second Temple, before they and it were immortalized on the Arch of Titus in the Roman Forum. Am I privy to frozen time, annihilated time, transcended time, repeated time, or born-again time? Does this imposing menorah prove that the Jewish people have surmounted this political rupture thanks to the existence of the State of Israel? Or on the contrary does its very presence prove that they still cannot overcome it and continue to live in fear that it may be repeated?

The long concourse leading to the departure hall is covered with reproductions of Jewish Agency posters spanning the years both before and after the creation of Israel, posters meant to kick off its annual campaigns on behalf of the Jewish settlement. The first posters go back to the 1930s. The menorah is ubiquitous in all of them. It contemplates the efforts of the first pioneers who tilled a harsh land; those who built the cranes that serviced the ports; those who created the first airline fleet; the first youth organizations; the first military battalions; the first hospitals; the first kindergartens and schools. Looking at the youth of the protagonists, their confident smiles as they look out toward a radiant future, one can easily think the concourse is devoted to Soviet nostalgia: same years, same hopes. A spectacular portrait of an Israel in the making whose epic efforts brought the state into existence, now turned into a distant past.

In the departure hall, the silver menorah, however, evokes far more ancient and complex worlds. I have the feeling that it is the instrument that activates the Stargate, opening it to the infinity of other worlds. Point it toward any of the destinations, and whoever crosses through it will be carried into other planets. Turn the menorah toward its origins and one is instantly transported back to the Moses in the desert, but also to the Ashkenazi rabbi who at the President's Conference refused all conversions. If you turn it toward the Temple Mount, you are instantly transported into the glorious epoch the extremists willing to blow up the Dome of the Rock seek to restore. Turn it toward Rome and one embarks on the long tale of diasporic suffering underpinning the official ideology of the state, so well incarnated by the license plates on the car of Israel's president. Put it on the bodybuilder's T-shirt and the menorah will incarnate everyday modernity. Transform it into an official logo on a diplomatic attaché case or on a uniform and it will incarnate state power. Paste it on a citrus fruit, and it will incarnate Israel's early agricultural ideals.

But put the menorah next to the Star of David, not the one that adorns the Israeli flag but the one that covers all the Torah mantles and the frontispieces of synagogues around the world, and the menorah will lose its power and intensity. The Star of David incarnates the religious emotion and continuity of the Jewish people who survived before the creation of the Israeli state in the four corners of the world—and who are slowly re-creating this global presence.

The ultraorthodox man with his hatbox taking the corridor toward the New York gate will be heading to his other home in Brooklyn in what is the continuation of his Israeli space . . . but he could just as easily head toward the Ukraine to pray on the tombs of his Hassidic saints, or to Hong Kong in his own community. The secular Israeli who was born in America with his attaché case and his cellphone will land among his professional peers in a New York City that has little in common with the city a left-wing Israeli-born academic seeks to integrate. The Lubavitch Rebbe heading out toward Mumbai may be in the same plane with the IT specialists heading out to Bangalore, but, not unlike Einstein's train passengers, they will not be traveling in the same space/time. Their portals will be different, and it is unclear whose past will be the other's future. The bodybuilder will display his muscles in a Russian competition, but he will not meet those former Soviet Jews who are returning to their ancient homeland for business deals. The historian of the Holocaust will travel to the same Berlin as the contemporary Israeli artist, but obsessed with the past he will not travel in the same circles as she who is obsessed with the wounds of the Israeli present. The Israeli tourist touring Europe on his holidays will not feel the same vibrations as the non-native Israeli citizen who returns to the land of his youth. And what is one to make of the left-wing Israeli journalist who has written the equivalent of a "Persian letter" from the calm of a Swedish island?[2] Is Israel the Bach of nations, uniquely able to invent its own infinite variations?

At the last minute, almost by miracle, all those non-Jewish others one has lost sight of in Israel converge at the gates, ready to take off for home: an Italian priest with his flock, a group of Armenian nuns, Protestant pilgrims, foreign diplomats, Asian tourists, Filipinos heading for home. They have of course walked on the same Israeli soil as the Jews, but on some other archeological layer and with a mental and geographic map guided by another North Star. Theirs are parallel itineraries without highway exchanges, for the Jewish vibrations and the internal historical codes, which despite its modernity continue to inhabit this departure hall, produce an inaudible sound to an outsider's ear. This is the same sound that will, sooner or later, induce most Israelis living abroad to return home, to their Land/Earth, in order to fully grasp it and to breathe freely its rarefied air.

Suddenly this metaphysical horizon darkens, and the "absolute other," the everyday neighbor, appears in the distance. At the duty-free exit, mundane as all others in the world where one buys alcohol, cigarettes, and perfumes, I notice two Arab Israeli women: an elderly one in a djellaba and her daughter in blue jeans, both wearing hijabs. They slowly head toward the flight that will take them to New York, where their son and brother is surely waiting for them, an Israeli not quite like the others, who has now joined the vast community of young Palestinians who have left these enigmatic lands where hope is wanting.

I am completely stunned by the presence of these two women. They stand there where one no longer expects to see them, not unlike miscast film extras stumbling into the wrong studio. They speak to each other in Arabic, and this language, which should be so familiar, given Israel's location, sounds terribly exotic as if it were little more than the garbled sounds captured by powerful antennas in search of distant stars. The two women walk slowly, holding on tightly to their newly bought perfumes, not unlike explorers in a vast terra incognita, anything but at home.

The Israeli Stargate, so powerfully open to other worlds and other space/times, suddenly becomes little more than a rear-view mirror with its inevitable blind spot, unable to see the fast-approaching earthly neighbor.

Last take.

EPILOGUE: ISRAEL *QUO VADIS?*

Throughout this book, I have referred to Israel's "move" in symbolic and psychological terms in order to describe a country that thought of itself well beyond its still contested borders. The time has come to ask: Where exactly is Israel "moving to"?

To a satellite in the middle of the Pacific Ocean, if one were to judge by the welcoming logo on the video screens of the 2012 Israeli "Facing Tomorrow" Presidential Conference. The eyes of the beholder zoomed in on the vast body of water halfway between the American West Coast on the right and the Chinese Coast on the left. No trace of Israel as a territorial entity, of the Middle East, of Europe, or even for that matter of the East Coast (as if Washington, D.C., were no longer relevant): Israel's future dematerialized.

If one returns instead to Israel's terrestrial dimension, one can ask with some provocation whether the entire country might not go through the Stargate of Ben-Gurion Airport. That would be the greatest hope of those extremist Islamists around the world for whom the Jews in Palestine are only impostors and usurpers who have broken the unity of the Muslim Ummah. On this count, charter flights would certainly be less apocalyptic that the classic rhetorical invocation of some Arabs and Muslims of "throwing the Jews into the sea."

A collective departure toward other horizons might just prove acceptable to an international community that, under the guidance of newly emerging powers and in the context of repeated economic crises, would have reverted to enlightened authoritarianism far from the humanist, democratic, and universal values of the old continents (in the plural to include all countries with a Western heritage).

It is easy to imagine that those Jews for whom Zionism consisted mainly in bringing these values to a sovereign Jewish people might choose to return to the West, be it European, North American, Australian, or even nowadays, Latin American. Such Israelis abroad could form Hebraic communities linked through the Internet and through constant travel, while being fully integrated in their respective democratic settings. Israel's academics and artists, businessmen and scientists, already so omnipresent in Europe and in America, would become the avant-gardes of such a movement. Europe, it goes without saying, would benefit more than others from such a move, which would bring a renaissance to its aging structures.

Nor should one forget the impressive group of secular Russians, not terribly concerned by democratic values and mainly interested in business with its frequent cortege of corruption. Such a group could move again, this time freely, to Birobidzhan, the autonomous region Stalin had "given" to the Jews in 1934. Near the Chinese border, thus at a stone's throw from the economic giant, this region would be center stage in a new planetary boom. It could become the last creative rampart of the "White" or at least "non-Han" man, with the Jews as active intermediaries, thanks to the numerous (new) Jewish communities that will one day emerge inside China itself.[1]

Nor should one exclude from such a "move" the ultraorthodox Jews. They will navigate around the globe and among continents as true experts, held together by their Law and its multiple compulsory practices, and totally indifferent to the diversity of political contexts. Their only concern: to be able to keep their identity, to live among themselves and according to their principles. This right, traditionally guaranteed by the Prince, will allow them to flourish under all types of intelligent authoritarian regimes.

Let there be no misunderstanding. I am not envisaging, much less advocating, the end of Israel, but instead imagining its evolution, its expansion beyond its current limits—an expansion that bears no connection to Tsahal's tanks but is the child of a vast Jewish and Israeli planetary movement based on constant travel and return trips. In such a scenario, Israel would became a base camp, an ongoing reference point, even a pied à terre, for the Jewish people, for barring catastrophes no Israeli or Jew in the world would ever want to definitively leave it. Life is meaningful and beautiful in Tel Aviv and in Jerusalem.[2] But in all three scenarios, there is no need to pursue the rhetoric of vast (and occupied) spaces. Like the new towers in Tel Aviv, Israel could think of itself as a vertical co-op with compact lands inside the Green Line.

As the saying goes, "one cannot have one's cake and eat it too." If, as I have tried to show in this book, fewer and fewer Israelis seriously envisage a two-state solution for the future—a wonderful and somewhat distracted mantra of an international community that never seriously gave itself the means to implement it with the necessary pressure—then one must confront a bitter truth: the current pleasant status quo (for Israeli Jews) cannot last forever.[3] History and people are always on the move, not necessarily in the ideal direction of peace and progress, but they are on the move.

Today's Israel, dashing toward the future with an incredible creative energy but also with a self-satisfaction bordering on hubris will not be able to endure in its current setting. The summer of tent protests and the autumn of United Nations votes in 2011 passed with no tangible results, before the current prolonged hibernation. But what will the future bring?

Some who belong to Israel's old left, so terribly marginalized since the end of the Oslo peace process, but now reinvigorated with new younger recruits, are beginning to evoke new solutions beyond the two-state vision. They are proposing confederal projects: two states united at the top by some kind of federal organism to strengthen the continuity between Jewish and Arab settlements. On this count they have Palestinian interlocutors who are thinking along similar lines.[4] No one harbors any illusions, however. The Israeli army, now fully penetrated bottom-up by religious nationalists, will not remove a single inhabitant from the smallest settlement in "Judea and Samaria." The shock of what happened in Gaza after Israel's withdrawal has destroyed the prospects of any similar policy in the West Bank. The dream of Ramallah with its start-up nation is also slowly disappearing because Palestine is dissolving into an ever more confined and patchy space. Besides, who would want a country without territorial contiguity? The example of Nagorno-Karabakh is hardly encouraging. As a result the country may be entering into a war of attrition.[5]

A confederation? Israel is not Switzerland. One can only hope that no one will try to recreate a setting worthy of the Dayton Accords, a lame solution imposed by Richard Holbrooke in order to put an end to the bloody Yugoslav wars, but in a manner that went against every postwar European principle. Bosnia was organized politically along three ethnic and confessional lines: Croat Catholic, Serb Orthodox, and Bosnian Muslim as three Legos of a still tottering artificial edifice. The outcome was worthy of Europe's worst prewar specters: Jakob Finci, a Jewish citizen of Sarajevo, who during the civil war presided over the newly rebuilt Jewish charity organization, La Benevolencia, that delivered first aid, food, and medicines in all sectors of the besieged city, was unable to run for president of the Bosnian Confederation, despite his wide popularity in the country, because he belonged to none of its three official ethnic-religious groups.[6]

If no political solution is found to enable Israelis and Palestinians to live together, who will remain on these contested lands? The Israeli ultranationalists will stay on, faithful to the Masada tradition, with the fortress becoming once again the last rampart of an existential "no" rather than a sublime opera set for trendy cosmopolitans. The ultrareligious nationalists can even find a modus vivendi with their Muslim equivalents around the burning bush. Buttressed by their Torah and their Koran, they can then invoke what an ultrareligious philosopher told me recently, namely, that Ishmael and Isaac buried their father Abraham together. In terms of daily life, these ultrareligious can get along, given their common desire to seclude men and women in ever more separate and rigid contexts. I am also told that these two groups now share the same tram and often buy staples in the same low-cost shops . . . perhaps as involuntary partners in a new grassroots daily life in twenty-first-century Jerusalem, although other accounts are far less optimistic.[7]

But what about all the others? All those who do not have the privilege of possessing a second passport, who are not sufficiently educated to aspire to ever more globalized careers and opportunities, who have no access to the elite scientific corps of the army with their concomitant protection from the dangers of the front, or who cannot enter the lofty realm of Israeli cyberspace? Simple foot soldiers of a static situation, they have inherited the choices made by their parents, grandparents, and now even great-grandparents to move to Israel in order to live in a normal state. But this long-sought-for normality is still elusive.[8]

Will they want to live in a pied à terre? Will they accept to blend inside the region with the hope of one day being able to travel across it through a renewed Stargate linked to the ancient glorious pasts of a Jewish presence at the heart of the Arab world? Will they leave the country to return "home" to the West? Will they bring Israel toward a new, far more ethnic, Asian horizon? No one can portend the future.

I have written this book with all of these nonprivileged Israelis in mind, in the hope that they may through their political participation bring Israel back to its earlier modesty and its humanistic values, before it is too late.

NOTES

INTRODUCTION

Note: All translations are mine, unless otherwise noted.

1. The boycott was covered extensively. See, for instance, Robert Daniel, "Tempest in a Tub: Israel's Cottage Cheese Wars," *Wall Street Journal,* June 16, 2011.

2. This change in attitude was on display during the Third President's Conference (which I will describe in greater detail in note 10) held in Jerusalem in June 2011. One of the leading roundtables was titled "Israel and America: Has the Love Cooled?" (June 22). The entire program can be found at www.presidentconf.org.il/2011/en.

3. Thomas Friedman, *The World Is Flat: A Brief History of the Twenty-First Century* (New York: Farrar, Straus and Giroux, 2005).

4. How to perpetuate the Israeli identity of the children of these Israeli expatriates is beginning to preoccupy national policy analysts. In his paper "Strengthening Jewish-Israeli Identity of Israelis Abroad," published by the Jewish People's Policy Institute (JPPI), March 22, 2012, Yogev Karasenty suggests creating Israeli youth movements abroad, Houses of Israeli culture, Israeli schools, and absentee ballots for elections, and, most significant of all, "improving Israel's *image*" (emphasis added). The paper can be found at www.jppi.org.il.

5. "Israel Hits 7.2 Billion Dollars in Army Exports," www.upi .com, June 17, 2011. This sum was also reported in an Israeli website appropriately titled www.spacewar.com ("Israel's Military Exports Reach 7.2 Billion Dollars," June 17, 2011).

6. This attitude was best summarized in a timely article by Bradley Burston, "The Holocaust Means Never Having to Say You Are

Sorry," *Haaretz,* June 5, 2012. The author places Israel's military overreaction to the flotilla seeking to challenge the Gaza blockade in a wider perspective. Israeli elite units preemptively raided the Turkish ship, the *Marmara*, on May 31, 2010, killing several Turks in the process.

7. The Christian Hebraists in the seventeenth century inaugurated this biblical reflection in the Netherlands; Oliver Cromwell gave it a clear republican twist in Great Britain. In our times, eminent political philosophers such as Michael Walzer have given new life to biblical political thought as a vital element of political theory. But in terms of daily politics in Israel, the political thought emanating from the Torah is to be found mainly among the ultrareligious right. See Michael Walzer, Menachem Lorberbaum, Noam J. Zohar, and Yair Lorberbaum, eds., *The Jewish Political Tradition,* 2 vols. (New Haven: Yale University Press, 2000, 2003).

8. Anna Foa makes this argument in her *The Jews of Europe after the Black Death* (Berkeley: University of California Press, 2000).

9. For a detailed analysis of the contrast between the European "never again" and the Jewish "never again," see my "Europe and Israel Today: Can Their Incompatible 'Never Again(s)' Be Reconciled?," in *The Liberal-Republican Quandary in Israel, Europe and the United States: Early Modern Thought Meets Current Affairs,* ed. Thomas Maissen and Fania Oz-Salzberger (Brighton, MA: Academic Studies Press, 2012). An earlier version appeared in French as " 'Plus jamais ça' Europe-Israel: Les malentendus,' " *Le Débat,* no. 161 (September–October 2010): 144–157.

10. I was able to experience firsthand this change of film scenarios when I participated in the June 2011 President's Conference in Jerusalem, hosted by Israeli president Shimon Peres. These yearly Davos-like meetings bring together Jewish and Israeli political, business, intellectual, and scientific elites to discuss the theme of "Facing Tomorrow." In June 2011, during a plenary session on "Global Perspectives for Tomorrow," the public of several hundred participants remained in stony silence without the slightest applause when Denis Ross, the American diplomat who worked most fervently for an

Israeli-Palestinian peace process, announced that he was bringing the good tidings and warmest wishes of President Obama. The participants instead gave an ovation to the Chinese minister of culture, who was welcomed like a grand dignitary from another epoch, after he delivered a diplomatically rigid and set speech on China's national identity and quest for international harmony based on traditional Confucian values.

1. THE INTERGALACTIC CAFÉ, OR BEN-GURION AIRPORT

1. The persons I mention here are all members of the "Haredi" world (commonly defined as "black" because of their dress codes). Beyond that, it is virtually impossible to provide clear definitions of the Jewish and Israeli orthodox and ultraorthodox worlds. The lines separating different "Haredi" Jews from the "Dati Leumi" (the national religious Zionists) and the modern orthodox, not to mention the Lubavichers, are increasingly blurred. New permutations are always emerging inside a rapidly changing Israeli society where religious identities, nationalist feelings, and social and political choices seem to constantly recombine as in a kaleidoscope. I was confirmed in this impression by several orthodox and ultraorthodox Jews who all stressed that nowadays they too have difficulties drawing clear identity lines among their own groups.

2. The sea of Russian flags that greeted Vladimir Putin in Jerusalem on his first trip to Israel on June 25, 2012, exemplified the strong ties that now exist between the two countries and their peoples, one of history's most rapid turnabouts when one remembers the "Free Soviet Jewry" movement that was the rallying cry of the entire Jewish world in the 1970s and 1980s.

3. Nurit Anderman, "Reveling in Her Roles: Actress Hiam Abbass Turns Director and Scriptwriter in New Film *Hajar*," *Haaretz,* August 16, 2011.

4. For a good description of this particular sense of belonging, see Salman Masalha, "The Nakba Is Alive for Both Jews and Arabs," *Haaretz,* May 31, 2012.

5. For a glimpse inside the life of Israeli Arabs, see Susan Nathan, *The Other Side of Israel: My Journey across the Israel-Arab Divide* (London: HarperPerennial, 2006).

6. On July 18, 2012, Mydia Wietzman, the foreign press adviser to the Israeli Ministry of Tourism, announced: "3 Million People Viewed the Ministry of Tourism's Website in Chinese during Its First Week." Sent by israeltourismministry@gmail.com. The Chinese site can be seen at http://weibo.com/igto.

7. "David Ben-Gurion: A Brief Biography and Quotes" can be found at http://www.palestineremembered.com/Acre/Famous-Zionist-Quotes/Story638.html.

8. Israel chose to deport some South Sudanese illegal immigrants in June 2012, given diplomatic relations between the two countries, but the vast majority of illegal immigrants could not be deported under international law because they faced repression if they returned to their lands of origin. The fence built along the Egyptian border is designed to prevent further immigration while also protecting Israel from the lawlessness of the Sinai desert. See Isabel Kershner, "Crackdown on Migrants Tugs at Soul of Israelis," *New York Times,* June 18, 2012.

2. THE TWO ROADS TO JERUSALEM

1. For a full presentation of the history of this route, see B'Tselem, http://www.btselem.org/freedom_of_movement/checkpoints_and_forbidden_roads, and the website of the Association of Civil Rights in Israel, http://www.acri.org.il/en/2010/05/25/route-443fact-sheet-and timeline.

2. Nevertheless, see the op-ed by Alain Salomon and Katia Salomon, "A Morning at an Israeli Checkpoint," *International Herald Tribune,* March 30, 2011.

3. For two contradictory accounts on the meaning of this decision, see Matthew Ackerman, "The *Altalena*'s Enduring Power," *Commentary,* May 8, 2011, and Nathan Jeffay, "Israel Plans to Raise the Famed *Altalena*," *Forward,* August 3, 2011. For a dissenting Israeli perspective, see "Raising the *Altalena*," *Haaretz,* June 26, 2011.

3. The Lesson from East Talpiot

1. See Aviezer Ravitsky's pathbreaking work *Messianism, Zionism, and Jewish Religious Radicalism* (Chicago: University of Chicago Press, 1996).

2. Ravitsky's career as a professor at the Hebrew University was cut short by a terrible traffic accident that left him alive but intellectually incapacitated. Beyond his academic credentials, he was also a frequent guest lecturer in the American and European Jewish communities' circuit, where he was fond of using the "inherited grandchildren" story.

3. See Or Rosenberg, "Israeli Female Soldier Accosted for Rebuffing Haredi Bus Segregation," *Haaretz*, December 28, 2011; Ethan Bronner and Isabel Kershner, "Israelis Facing a Seismic Rift over Role of Women," *Haaretz*, January 14, 2012.

4. Associated Press, "Ultra-Orthodox Jews Blur Women with Modesty Glasses," *Huffington Post*, September 14, 2012, http://www.huffingtonpost.com/2012/08/08/ultra-orthodox-jews-blurry-glasses_n_1757338.html.

5. Amos Oz, "We Are All Brethren," *Haaretz*, August 2, 2011.

6. Anschel Pfeiffer, "New IDF Artillery Corps Created for Ultra-Orthodox Conscripts," *Haaretz*, August 2, 2011.

7. Ophir Bar Zohar, "Israeli Advocacy Group Urges Haredi Draft Must Not Be at the Expense of Women Soldiers," *Haaretz*, May 31, 2012. The centennial Women's International Zionist Organization (WIZO) worried most about the promotion of female officers in an army with many all-male battalions.

8. Charlemagne had begun the diplomatic exchange by sending to Baghdad in 797 a delegation that included one Jew from Narbonne in southern France, but it was Harun-el-Rachid's return delegation to Aix-la-Chapelle in 802 that came to epitomize the shift in geopolitical power. See http://www.jewishencyclopedia.com/articles/4250-charlemagne.

9. He is not alone in this excessively optimistic reading. See Isabel Kershner, "Silicon Valley Dreams Grow on the West Bank," *International Herald Tribune*, July 31, 2012.

10. Dan Senor and Saul Singer, *Start-Up Nation: The Story of Israel's Economic Miracle* (New York: Twelve, 2009).

11. Danny Rubinstein, "One State/Two States: Rethinking Israel and Palestine," *Dissent,* Summer 2010, www.dissentmagazine.org/article /?article=3254.

12. Dino Buzzati, *The Tartar Steppe* (London: Canongate Books, 2007). The original Italian edition was published in 1940.

13. Amos Oz, *The Hill of Evil Counsel* (London: Chatto and Windus, 1978).

14. Danny Rubenstein, "A Palace Befitting the Ruler of the Land," *Haaretz,* December 24, 2006.

15. Ezra Halevi, "Haaretz Editor Refuses to Retract Israel Apartheid Statements," *Arutz Asheva,* Israel National News, May 9, 2007.

16. James Cameron and Simcha Jacobovici coauthored a controversial documentary produced by the BBC in 2007. Its title: *The Lost Tomb of Jesus.* The full title of the conference: "The Third Princeton Theological Seminary Symposium on Jewish Views of the Afterlife and Burial Practices in Second Temple Judaism: Evaluating the Talpiot Tomb in Context" (Jerusalem, January 2008). The conference participants took the view that there was only a very small probability the ossuary belonged to Jesus's family. But it is hard to dispel the feeling that no one really wanted to delve into the matter thoroughly, for the stakes remain quite simply unimaginable.

17. One only needs to do a Google search on the phrase "Jesus family tomb" or "Oded Golan" to see just how passionate the debate has remained. The stakes go well beyond the historical or archeological givens of the issue.

4. IN THE EYE OF THE STORM

1. For a rapid overview of the soft drink question, see http://www .snopes.com/cokelore/israel.asp.

2. Hector Hoornaert, *Terre promise et Palestine moderne* (Paris: Les Éditions Vermaut, 1914), p. 194. A prefacing page indicates that the text had been "seen and approved" by the Bishop of Bruges on March

19, 1914. Hoornaert's description of the Jews reflects the prejudices of his time.

3. For a clear and concise explanation of the Tal Law's origins and the complexity of drafting ultraorthodox men into the military, see the Wikipedia entry "Tal Committee." The Tal Law expired on August 2, 2012, and as I write, there seems to be no political consensus on how to replace it. See Daniel Goldman, "The Tal Law's Real Winners and Losers," *Jerusalem Post,* August 2, 2012.

4. A quick Google search on the phrase "red heifer" will show that many of the entries, besides those of the Temple Institute, come from Christian groups who believe Christ's Second Coming will take place only after the physical reconstruction of the Temple.

5. By pure chance I saw the black presidential car on Route 443 in June 2011. The chauffeur had just accompanied President Shimon Peres to the airport and was returning alone without escort to Jerusalem, when my Moroccan chauffeur pointed out to me with great pride the speeding vehicle with its very special menorah car plate. I don't know whether the chauffeur would have taken that contested highway with the president on board.

6. I am here reproducing freely the gist of what was said by the rabbi who led the virtual video tour of the Temple esplanade. One can listen to his entire comments on the group's website by clicking on the video tour at www.templeinstitute.org.

7. Hoornaert, *Terre promise,* p. 196. I have made minute stylistic changes in my translation.

8. Ibid, p. 197

9. Gérard Fredj, "Le roi Hérode n'a pas pu achever la construction du Temple," *Israël-Infos,* no. 1033 (November 24, 2011). This article assumes that the Wall was finished slightly later. But to follow the controversy surrounding the dating of the Wall and its meaning, one need only turn to the countless entries posted on Google under the heading "Post-Herodian Wailing Wall?," most handling the topic in an ideological anti-Israeli vein. For a serious take on the question in a Palestinian publication from the Institute for Palestine Studies, one that underscores traditional Jewish ambivalence over worshipping at the Wall,

see Simone Ricca, "Heritage, Nationalism and the Shifting Symbolism of the WailingWall," *Jerusalem Quarterly* 6, no. 1 (Summer 2005): 39–56. It is to be found under www.jerusalemquarterly.org/images / . . . 24_ricca.

10. Moshe Halbertal, *People of the Book: Canon, Meaning, and Authority* (Cambridge, MA: Harvard University Press, 1997); Halbertal, *Concealment and Revelation: Esotericism in Jewish Thought and Its Philosophical Implications,* trans. Jackie Feldman (Princeton: Princeton University Press, 2007); Halbertal, with Avishai Margalit, *Idolatry* (Cambridge, MA: Harvard University Press, 1998). His most recent book is *On Sacrifice* (Princeton: Princeton University Press, 2012). The Shalom Hartman Institute in Jerusalem is one of the centers of this modern orthodox renewal, which is opposed to the idolatry implicit in the pre-rabbinical Judaism preached by the founders of the Temple Institute.

11. Hoornaert, *Terre promise,* pp. 235–236.

12. Ibid., p. 237.

5. Rooted Utopias

1. Finfacts Team, "Israel Has 71 Companies on NASDAQ Stock Exchange; Ireland Has 7," *Finfacts: Business and Finance Portal,* January 7, 2006.

2. Hebrew University of Jerusalem, *The Hebrew University Lab: Research Today for a Better Tomorrow,* brochure distributed at the Third President's Conference, Jerusalem, June 2011. There is a short YouTube presentation under the same title.

3. This scientific thesis was given mass-media attention with the international success of Hubert Sauper's documentary film "Darwin's Nightmare," which was released in 2005.

4. Prof. Yigal Erel, "Cross-Border Pollution in the Middle East," p. 51 of the *Hebrew University Lab* brochure.

5. David Grossmann, "Why? Who Died?," *Haaretz,* February 24, 2012. Hebrew original: http://www.haaretz.co.il/news/politics /1.1649589. Translated by Sol Salbe of the Middle East News Ser-

vice, Melbourne, Australia, https://www.facebook.com/profile.php?id =523794418*.

6. Walid Selem, "La sourde et étrange colère d'un Libanais face au film 'Lebanon,'" *Rue 89,* April 2, 2010.

7. Yosef Hayim Yerushalmi, "Servants of Kings and Not Servants of Servants: Some Aspects of the Political History of the Jews," 2005 Tenenbaum Lecture, given at the Tam Institute for Jewish Studies at Emory University, Atlanta, Georgia. There is a published edition in French as *Serviteurs des rois et non serviteurs des serviteurs* (Paris: Allia, 2011).

8. Aesaf Shtull-Trauning, "Laying Tefillim on a Cybernetic Arm: A Brave New World of Jewish Halakha," *Haaretz,* May 30, 2012.

9. Jessica Ganzi, "Premier jour, premier pas dans la Silicon Wadi," www.girlzinweb.com, June 21, 2011.

10. Cecilia Gabizon, "Israël: Nouvel Eldorado des start-up," *Le Figaro,* July 14, 2011.

11. To cite just two articles among many: "Peace Now: Israel Began Building 1851 New Houses in West Bank in 2011," *Haaretz,* January 10, 2012; "Israel Approves 277 Apartments in West Bank," *International Herald Tribune,* August 16, 2011.

6. THE AQUARIUM

1. This fear of suicide bombers has not entirely disappeared. It is only beginning to be addressed openly. See Eetta Prince-Gibson, "Touring Terror in Jerusalem," *International Herald Tribune,* August 22, 2012.

2. Menachem Klein, *The Shift: Israel/Palestine from Border Struggle to Ethnic Conflict* (New York: Columbia University Press, 2010).

3. David Dean Shulman has written an account of his early political engagement, *Dark Hope: Working for Peace in Israel and Palestine* (Chicago: University of Chicago Press, 2007).

4. David Dean Shulman, "Salt March to the Sea," *Harper's Magazine* (June 2011): 76–79.

5. For a direct response against the loyalty oath, see Amos Schocken, "The Necessary Elimination of Israeli Democracy," *Haaretz*, November 25, 2011.

6. Aziz Aby Sarah, "What Is Normal about Normalization?," *Haaretz*, December 26, 2011.

7. THE BUBBLE

1. For a glimpse at the complexity of these restrictions and the use of science to solve some issues, see Elie Dolgin, "A (Kosher) Can of Worms: Rabbis Go to the Museum to Probe Kashrut of Tiny Worms and Fish," *Forward*, August 14, 2012.

2. "You Haven't Seen Anything Yet: Top of Jaffa," advertisement, *Haaretz*, June 24, 2011, p. 3.

3. Irit Rosenblum, "Forget the Strife: Lonely Planet Puts Tel Aviv in Top Three Cities in the World," *Haaretz*, November 2, 2010.

4. For an introduction to Bartana's work, see Joshua Simon, "Yael Bartana: And Europe Will Be Stunned," on the website of the review *Domus*, www.domusweb.it, August 7, 2011. Also Carol Zemel, "The End(s) of Irony: Yael Bartana at the Venice Biennale, for Poland," *Forward*, July 15, 2011.

5. Bartana's manifesto was printed in poster format and stacked in large piles at the Polish Pavilion of the Biennale. Visitors could take it freely. The poster has a red background, the letters are in black, the Polish eagle and the Star of David in the background are in white.

6. Since the 2011 Biennale, Yael Bartana has pursued her work by turning it into a real-life artistic/political movement, which took place during the Seventh Berlin Biennale, May 11–13, 2012, at the KW Institute for Contemporary Art in Berlin. "Yael Bartana: The First International Congress of the Jewish Renaissance Movement in Poland at the Berlin Biennial," www.artiscontemporary.org/agenda_detail.php ?id=662.

7. "Art Biennale, Interview with Sigalit Landau, 2011," YouTube, www.youtube.com/watch?v=NBFDedy1gH0.

8. THE TENT

1. "On Thin Ice: Criticism versus Loyalty in Israel-Diaspora Relations," President's Conference, June 22, 2011; for the entire proceedings, see www.presidentconf.org.il/.

2. Rabbi Eric H. Yoffie, president of the Union of Reformed Judaism; Fania Oz-Salzberger, professor of political science, Faculty of Law, University of Haifa.

3. The term "the love of Israel" *(Ahavat Israel)* has a long theological pedigree. Gershon Sholem evoked it most powerfully when he accused Hannah Arendt of not displaying "love of Israel" for her criticisms of the Jewish Councils (the Judenrat) in occupied Europe for having facilitated the work of the Nazis in carrying out the Final Solution. Arendt had made these observations in her *Eichmann in Jerusalem* (New York: Viking Press, 1963).

4. See note 9. My article, "'Plus jamais ça' Europe, Israël: Les malentendus," *Le Débat,* no. 161 (September–October 2010): 144–157, was at its inception a paper originally delivered at the conference "Liberalism and Republicanism, Past and Present: Can Early Modern Concepts Address Current Affairs?," University of Haifa, Law Faculty, January 2–4, 2010.

5. Jeremy Ben-Ami, *A New Voice for Israel* (New York: Palgrave MacMillan, 2011).

6. Isi Liebler, "Candidly Speaking: J Street's Soft Sell for the Uninformed," *Jerusalem Post,* August 8, 2011.

7. Boaz Fyler, "Yesha Council Head: Time to Join Hands," Ynetnews.com, August 9, 2011, http://www.ynetnews.com/articles /0,7340,L-4106482,00.html.

8. Yossi Sarid, "Lebensraum as a Justification for Israeli Settlements," *Haaretz,* August 26, 2011.

9. Sari Nusseibeh, "Jeremy Ben-Ami's *A New Voice for Israel,*" *Washington Post,* August 4, 2011.

10. Jodi Rudoren, "In Israel, a Pursuit of Pragmatism," *International Herald Tribune,* August 18–19, 2012; Dany Dayan, "Israel's Settlers Are Here to Stay," *International Herald Tribune,* July 25, 2012.

11. "Conversion: Who Keeps the Gate for the Jewish Nation?," Israeli Presidential Conference, June 23, 2011. The participants: Gilan Dror, Peter Knobel, Dov Maimon, Ya'akov Ne'eman, Shmul Rosner (moderator), Natan Sharansky, and Eli Yshai.

12. Tomer Zarchin and Gidi Weitz, "A Glimpse at the Life of Israel's Controversial Justice Minister," *Haaretz,* January 8, 2011; Yair Ettinger, "Justice Minister: Rabbinical Courts Should Support Not Replace Civil Courts," *Haaretz,* December 8, 2009.

13. See the Wikipedia article "Israeli Law," http://en.wikipedia .org/wiki/Israeli_law.

14. If one googles the phrase "Jewish gene," one finds a long list of articles, some jubilatory, others with political overtones, still others that seem partially scientific, and a few that seem more serious. Sourcewise, the topic is much too moot to be treated as science.

15. Shlomo Sand, *The Invention of the Jewish People* (London: Verso, 2009).

16. Haaretz Service, "Could the Taliban Be Genetically Linked to the Jews?," *Haaretz,* January 14, 2010. The article does not specify whether this "gene" is maternal or paternal.

17. Pinto, " 'Plus jamais ça,' " note 9.

18. The video of Dr. Dov Maimon's presentation at the roundtable can be seen at www.jppi.org.il.

19. At the antipodes of this analysis, one need only think of academic feminist readings of Sinai, which argue on behalf of gender equality; cf. Judith Plaskow, *Standing Again at Sinai: Judaism from a Feminist Perspective* (San Francisco: HarperCollins, 1991).

9. BETWEEN MEMORY AND MEMORY CHIP

1. Yehuda Amichai, "Jerusalem, Jerusalem, Why Jerusalem?," in his last collection of poetry, *Open Closed Open,* trans. Chana Bloch and Chana Kronfeld (New York: Harcourt, 2000), p. 138.

2. Yitzak Fritz Bauer, whose book *Galut* played a pathbreaking role in German Jewish and Zionist consciousness when it appeared in 1936, was one of the founders of the Jewish History Department at

the Hebrew University of Jerusalem. Julius Guttmann, who wrote *The Philosophy of Judaism: The History of Jewish Philosophy from Biblical Times to Franz Rosenzweig,* was one of the founders of the Jewish Philosophy Department. The two men, just like Gerschom Scholem, had been formed in the context of the German Wissenschaft des Judentums, but they rebelled against its rational and scientifically neutral principles in the belief that this school was favoring the loss of Jewish identity through massive intellectual and cultural assimilation. Hence their Zionism and their choice to settle in the Yishuv in the 1920s and 1930s.

3. In a special issue of the French review *Le Débat* titled "History Captured by Fiction," Pierre Nora wonders whether the growing hybridization of history and fiction does not spell the end of History as the Muse of the past: Pierre Nora, "Histoire et roman: Où passent les frontières?," *Le Débat,* no. 165 (May–August 2011): 12.

4. *Zachor* is not just a major work of history but also a highly important autobiographical personal reflection on the condition of the Jewish historian. Yosef Hayim Yerushalmi, *Zakhor* (Seattle: University of Washington Press, 1982).

5. I am referring here to the groundbreaking writings of Ilan Pappé, Benny Morris, Idith Zertal, and Avi Shlaim, whose impact has been far greater in international historical debates than within the context of Israel's political debates. Ilan Pappé, *The Making of the Arab-Israeli Conflict, 1947–1951* (London: Tauris, 1994) and *The Ethnic Cleansing of Palestine* (New York: Oneworld, 2007); Benny Morris, *The Birth of the Palestinian Refugee Problem, 1947–1949* (Cambridge: Cambridge University Press, 1989) and *Righteous Victims: A History of the Zionist-Arab Conflict, 1881–2001* (New York: Vintage, 2001); Idith Zertal, *Israel's Holocaust and the Politics of Nationhood* (Cambridge: Cambridge University Press, 2010) and, with Akiva Eldar, *Lords of the Land: The War over Israeli Settlements in the Occupied Territories 1967–2007* (New York: Nation Books, 2007); Avi Shlaim, *The Iron Wall and the Arab World* (New York: W. W. Norton, 2001).

6. Friedlander's book disturbed his peers (both Jewish and German and the historical profession in general) by its desire to show that

the Jews had reacted against the Nazi threat and had thus played a role, minimal as it might be, in shaping their own destiny. At any rate their lived experiences during the Holocaust had to be integrated into the history of the period to provide a full understanding of the horrors of the epoch. See the interview that appeared in *Der Spiegel* on October 8, 2007, right before Friedlander was awarded the German Book Publishers' Prize. Also see Dominick La Capra, "Historical and Literary Approaches to the 'Final Solution': Saul Friedlander and Jonathan Littel," *History and Theory* 50, no. 1 (February 2011): 71–97.

7. At the end of his presentation Rabbi Sacks was given an ovation by the conference's attendees, who were all too happy to be comforted in their sense of never-ending antisemitic fear.

8. Chief Rabbi Sacks repeated this line of reasoning when commenting the debate over Jewish circumcision brought about by a German court that decreed it was illegal in terms of the child's human rights; "The Europeans' Skewed View of Circumcision," *Jerusalem Post*, July 5, 2012.

9. Those left-wing Israelis who feel responsible for what Israel has done to the Palestinians are marginalized, when not ostracized, in national debates, and even perceived as potential traitors in Israel's struggles. Gideon Levy's articles in *Haaretz* routinely provoke such reactions. And of course this problem of there being no sense of responsibility for state actions was particularly visible during the *Marmara* incident with Turkey, when the ship trying to break Gaza's blockade was intercepted with full military force, leading to several deaths.

10. Julia Lovell develops this theory in her most recent book, *The Opium Wars: Drugs, Dream, and the Making of China* (London: Picador, 2011).

11. Marcus Dysch, "*The Promise* Has an Anti-Israel Premise," *Jewish Chronicle*, February 24, 2011. The *Jewish Chronicle*, a respected independent Jewish weekly in London often cited in the media's press reports, also published a long interview with the filmmaker: "Interview: Peter Kosminsky," *Jewish Chronicle*, February 3, 2011.

12. Neville Rigby, "Epic Series, 'The Promise' Dramatizes Palestine, Past and Present," *Electronic Intifada*, April 15, 2011.

13. Roger Heacock, "Locating and Opening Palestinian Archives: A National Priority," Birzeit University Working Paper 2011/2012 (ENG).

14. The most illustrious voice on the Palestinian side is that of Sari Nusseibeh. He has argued for limited Palestinian rights in an open Israeli-Palestinian space in his *What Is a Palestinian State Worth?* (Cambridge, MA: Harvard University Press, 2011). On the Israeli side, Avraham Burg has argued for full social equality between Israelis and Palestinians with the creation of his political party, *Shivyon Yisrael,* and his critiques of the current Israeli government. See his "Now It Is Your Turn," *Haaretz,* December 12, 2011.

15. For extensive coverage of this theme, see Gilbert Achcar, *The Arabs and the Holocaust* (New York: Metropolitan Books, 2009).

16. Tom Segev analyzes this Israeli attitude in his *The Seventh Million: The Israelis and the Holocaust* (New York: Hill and Wang, 1994).

17. The Council of Europe has been instrumental in endorsing the teaching of the Holocaust in its member states across Europe (see Jean-Michel Lecomte, *Teaching about the Holocaust in the 21st Century,* Council of Europe publication, January 2001), as well as organizing Holocaust Remembrance Days, most often on January 27, the anniversary of the liberation of Auschwitz.

18. The most important exchange of letters between the two camps took place in the pages of the *New York Review of Books.* Twenty-nine prestigious Israeli signatories supported Yad Vashem's actions; see, for instance, Aharon Applefeld, Shlomo Avineri, Yehuda Bauer, and A. B. Yeshoua, "Bruno Schulz' Wall Paintings," *New York Review of Books,* May 23, 2002. This letter was a response to a previous letter signed by twenty-four American academics who defended Ukraine's right to keep the frescoes in the name of a pluralist vision of Central and Eastern Europe. The prestigious Israeli signatories were shocked at the very idea that either Poland or the Ukraine had ever given much importance or thought to the Jewish populations on their lands. This original letter, referred to in the Israeli reply as having being published in the *New York Review of Books* on November 29, 2001, does not appear in the *Review*'s electronic index. But four of its original signatories

replied to the Israeli letter in the same May 23 issue by stressing that the "pluralism" to which they had referred was not the missing one of the past but the one that was beginning to emerge after the fall of communism. The entire exchange was thus a perfect illustration of the battle between past and future.

19. Ethan Bronner, "Behind Fairy Tale Drawings, Walls Speak of Unspeakable Cruelty," *New York Times,* February 27, 2009.

10. STARGATE

1. I found this paragraph in the French Wikipedia article on *Stargate,* http://fr.wikipedia.org/wiki/Stargate, which I consulted on September 19, 2011. The paragraph does not exist in the *Stargate* entry of the English Wikipedia.

2. Gideon Levy, "Island of Sanity," *Haaretz,* June 24, 2011, pp. 20–21.

EPILOGUE

1. The first Limmud meeting in China, bringing together Jews to study and socialize around Jewish themes, took place in Beijing in early June 2012. There are currently 6,000 Jews living in China and more than 20,000 living in Asia. Clive Lawton, "After China It Is Now Official: Limmud Is Now a Global Phenomenon," *Haaretz,* June 8, 2012.

2. In 2012, *Lonely Planet* considered Tel Aviv among the top ten "ultimate party cities": Reuven Weiss, "Lonely Planet: Tel Aviv among Top Ten 'Ultimate Party' Cities," Ynetnews.com, August 6, 2012, http://www.ynetnews.com/articles/0,7340,L-4265070,00.html. In 2011, it ranked Tel Aviv the third-best city in the world. As for Jerusalem, its breakfast spots are apparently among the best in the world: Daniela Dean, "Smart Mouth: The Delectable Nature of Israeli Breakfast," *Washington Post,* August 10, 2012.

3. On this count, see these diametrically opposing views: Avraham Burg, "Israel's Fading Democracy," *International Herald Tribune,* August 6, 2012; and Dany Dayan, "Israel's Settlers Are Here to Stay," *International Herald Tribune,* July 25, 2012.

4. See Sari Nusseibeh, *What Is a Palestinian State Worth?* (Cambridge, MA: Harvard University Press, 2011).

5. There is a new wind stirring in Palestinian lands as I write in August 2012. Many Palestinian activists now refuse to accept joint Israeli-Palestinian peace initiatives and protests, seeing them as nefarious accessories to "normalization"—that is, the daily acceptance of Israeli occupation. The most spectacular sign of this changed environment was the Palestinian refusal to have Daniel Barenboim's Diwan Orchestra (co-founded with Edward Said) play a concert as scheduled in East Jerusalem at the Mount of Olives. "Concert Nixed after Claims of 'Normalization,'" Associated Free Press, July 26, 2012.

6. Mark Lattimer, "The Saviour of Sarajevo Barred for Being a Jew," *Guardian*, April 22, 2010.

7. The interaction between Jewish and Arab residents of Jerusalem has not been easy since the official opening of the tramway. See Matthew Teller, "Jerusalem Tram Offers View of Other Side of the Track," November 5, 2011, www.BBC.co.uk.news/world-middle-east-15590267.

8. Peter Beinart, in *The Crisis of Zionism* (New York: Times Books, 2012), and Gershon Gorenberg, in *The Unmaking of Israel* (New York: HarperCollins, 2011), have both argued that Israel's normality was compromised by its victory in the 1967 war and its subsequent occupation of Palestinian lands. Without a two-state solution, they argue, no normality can ever be reached. Many critics consider these readings as too simplistic, because they presuppose that everything was normal and ideal before the 1967 war. See David Shulman, "Israel in Peril," *New York Review of Books*, June 7, 2012; and Jeffrey Goldberg, "Did Israel Actually Lose the 1967 War?," *New York Times*, November 18, 2011.

ACKNOWLEDGMENTS

I bore this book for many years without even knowing it. I am tempted to say that it wrote itself after two nearly consecutive academic trips to Jerusalem and Tel Aviv in June 2011. I had no intention to write these pages when I had the informal conversations with the persons I evoke in the book—conversations that I describe and that triggered within me that mixture of emotion and angst that forms the backbone of this book.

It is for this reason that I chose not to name my interlocutors. They did not know at the time, nor did I, that their statements would find their way into a book. Our conversations were not interviews, and I did not want their spontaneous impressions captured at a given moment to cast the least shadow on their writings or official functions. They, on the other hand, will easily recognize themselves and I thank them here for their precious insights and above all for having shared with me their fears and their hopes. Conversely, the persons I name and whose official declarations I conveyed were all expressing themselves in public contexts. I was not the only one to have heard their statements.

This book would not have been written without Pierre Nora's encouragement. He listened to my impressions when I returned from Israel and told me to "go home and write them down immediately to produce a 'Return from Israel' along the lines of André Gide's *Return from the Soviet Union*." The book was born out of this suggestion. I must thank here Marcel Gauchet for having introduced me to my French publisher, Stock, where I was greeted with the utmost kindness by François Azouvi, my editor, who agreed to take on an atypical manuscript and allowed it to become a book.

My friends Jean-François Bouthors, Dominique Danic-Careil, and Menachem Klein deserve special mention. They all read the initial manuscript with the greatest care and offered me their generous comments, moreover filling in the gaps respectively in my biblical, psychoanalytical, and Israeli political knowledge. My heartfelt thanks go out to them, with the proviso that I am of course uniquely responsible for any errors in the text.

Many other friends and colleagues either read the book in its French version or in my own English adaptation, offering me generous advice and suggestions in the preparation of the current edition. I list them here with the greatest of pleasures, and thank them individually for their kind help: Gisela Dachs, Sergio Della Pergola, Jean-Marc Dreyfus, Olivier Guez, Dick Howard, Orna Kenan, Ruth Kevess-Cohen, Rivon Krygier, Jean-Marc Liling, Dov Maimon, Michael Mertes, Miriam Rosen-Ayalon, Tony Smith, and Judith Vichniac. I am particularly grateful to Hélène and Jean-Manuel Bourgois, Saul Friedlander, Arthur Goldhammer, Eva Illouz, Cilly Kugelman, and Geoffrey Staines, and above all to Susan Neiman, for their unflagging support, constant encouragement, and piloting skills as I moved the book from its French base into uncharted English and German waters. Finally, special thanks go to Ian Malcolm, my English editor, for having welcomed my book at Harvard University Press, and to Henning Marmulla, my German editor, for having done the same at Suhrkamp. Their contagious enthusiasm encouraged me in the preparation of this updated edition.

One cannot be Jewish while writing in a somewhat critical and detached vein about Israel without experiencing a secret (and not so secret) fear of having gone "too far." My husband, Dominique Moïsi, encouraged me as I wrote and above all reassured me by scrutinizing all versions of the manuscript. Our sons, Luca and Laurent Moïsi, by their critiques forced me to modulate my thoughts more than once in order to take into account the view of their younger generation. They were all actively involved in a project that, by its essence, was as much existential as intellectual. Their support was indispensable.

I reserve the last thank you for Israel itself: its exuberant and contradictory society, its progress as well as its impasses, its euphoria as well as its depressions, its energy and its fears, and above all its simple existence, allowed me to seize in all of their complexities the vicissitudes of our world and our time.